POWELL
PRESSBURGER
AND OTHERS

Edited by Ian Christie

1978

Published by/British Film Institute/127 Charing Cross Road, London WC2H 0EA

Published in conjunction with the retrospective presented by Film
Availability Services, the National Film Archive and the National Film
Theatre, October-November 1978.

Cover: A publicity photograph from the production of *The Life and Death
of Colonel Blimp* (1943). Michael Powell making a stitch in the tapestry
used as background for the credits; with Emeric Pressburger, Deborah
Kerr, Alfred Junge and others (courtesy of the Rank Organisation and the
National Film Archive Stills Library).

contents

acknowledgments

Acknowledgment and thanks are due to the following: Ian Cameron for permission to reprint an article from *Movie*; Raymond Durgnat for his (pseudononymous) *Movie* article and a new essay specially written for this book; John Ellis for his specially written contribution; Thomas Elsaesser for permission to reprint his article from *Brighton Film Review*; *Positif* for permission to reprint Jean-Paul Török's review, and Tom Milne for his translation; Lawrence Hayward for advice on wartime propaganda and material in the Public Record Office. Transcripts of Crown copyright records in the Public Record Office appear by permission of the Controller of Her Majesty's Stationery Office.

At various stages in the preparation of this work, I have had the benefit of advice and assistance from: Roger Hewins and other former students and staff of Derby College of Art and Trent Polytechnic, Richard Collins, Charles Barr, Tony Rayns and Alan Howden (BBC TV). Among colleagues in the BFI who have been particularly helpful: Gillian Hartnoll, John Gillett and Peter Seward; David Francis, Jeremy Boulton, Michelle Snapes; Colin McArthur, David Meeker.

I am grateful to Deirdre McClosky, Patsy Nightingale and, especially, Paul Willemen for their patience, encouragement and help in assembling the book; and to Michael Powell and Emeric Pressburger for their co-operation.

I should like to dedicate this book to the Electric Cinema, Portobello Road, London, and to Peter Howden, for their devotion to the cause of Powell, Pressburger and others.

Introduction

Ian Christie

The aim of this book is not to offer a comprehensive evlauation of the work of Michael Powell and Emeric Pressburger — not only for the usual reasons of editorial modesty, lack of space, etc. — but because such a project would be altogether premature in the absence of any sustained discussion in recent years around the work and the issues it raises. It is hoped, therefore, that this may prove useful initially as a handbook and a stimulus to further analysis and research, which should be greatly helped by the National Film Theatre retrospective, screenings at Regional Film Theatres and elsewhere, and a BFI programme of bringing back into circulation many of the films long unavailable outside the National Film Archive viewing service.

A word about the strategy and organisation of the book. The title invites clarification in at least two ways: *which* others? and *why* others? 'Which' is answered partly by the *Chronicle* that follows, where careers and events whose trajectories intersect with those of Powell and Pressburger are traced in outline. This should stress the collaborative nature of their partnership, Powell's distinctive emphasis on 'teamwork' — not in the sense of a patronising *cameraderie,* but as an encouragement of distinct and even contradictory elements within the production ensemble — it should also evoke something of the precarious history of production in Britain. But then the question *why?* arises. Is this not simply to veer back toward a more sophisticated version of the familiar empiricist aesthetic that regards individual films as the product of multifarious skills and processes, with the director a more or less efficient 'conductor'? In point of fact, the Powell-Pressburger collaboration would seem to pose a challenge to the 'unreconstructed' *auteur* position. By signing their films jointly, whatever the division of responsibility, they denied the primacy of the individual artist; but at the same time their consolidation of production functions — as producers, writers and directors — was both the result of a pragmatic assessment of the best strategy to achieve a degree of autonomy and continuity within the fragile structure of the British film industry, and a bid to assume aesthetic control over production (two of Powell's reference points were Disney and Hitchcock).

But of course, the *auteur* theory was never 'on the side' of production. The *auteur* is not the director who appears *more* in control of his films than another; 'he' is more like a principle of coherence, a product of 'reading' certain films within a particular rubric, than a peculiarly gifted or fortunate director (although he may be these as well). The inscription of 'authorship', according to the *auteur* theory, in a group of films bearing the same signature is neither a matter of intentions realised nor of the director's fingerprints; although it can perhaps be accounted for 'because it is

1

through the force of his preoccupations that an unconscious, unintended meaning can be decoded in the film, *usually to the surprise of the individual involved*' (Peter Wollen[1]). This marks the passage to a 'modified' *auteur* theory, which insists on the methodological distinction between 'author' and *auteur*, although there often remains a persistent confusion between the concrete interviewable persons (Powell and Pressburger) and the 'structure' ('Powell/Pressburger'), deciphered from a study of their films. This confusion is further compounded by the tendency to use *auteur* terminology in a casual, descriptive way and by the deliberate conflation of *auteur* analysis with ascriptions of personal achievement in the practices of publicity and journalism.

A second area of confusion exists around the exclusiveness and scope of *auteur* theory. Wollen maintains that *auteur* analysis does not 'exhaust what can be said about any single film. It does no more than provide a way of decoding a film, by specifying what its mechanics are at one level'.[2] In principle, this should pave the way for other forms of analysis but, if it has rarely done so in practice, this may be because, as Stephen Heath claims,[3] *auteur* analysis cannot simply co-exist alongside other 'equally valid' approaches; it must either criticise or be criticised by them. This is not the place to pursue an extended review of the post-*auteur* debate: it will be enough to note that, gradually, attention has shifted from the problem of the 'author' to that of the 'reader', or spectator. 'The birth of the reader', as Barthes remarked, 'must be at the cost of the death of the Author'.[4] What matters is not so much the metaphysics of authorship as the need to resist the cultural dynamic which creates 'artists' or 'authors' as a means of delimiting research and fixing meaning in the frozen image of the artist's 'genius'. Historically, *auteur* theory proved to be an enormously productive phase in film and cultural studies, and it is apparent that many of its findings are of permanent value. But it seems equally clear today that this no longer holds true: the search for *auteurs* has become largely sterile, and the characterisation of films in terms of traditional *auteur* analysis is at the expense of what now appear to be more productive lines of inquiry.

Interestingly, *auteur* theory had little to say about British cinema — indeed one suspects that its dominance may have inhibited development of the necessary *historical* understanding. During the last twenty years, there has been a certain symmetry between, on the one hand, the advance of *auteur* analysis as applied to American cinema, with a corresponding lack of attention to the industrial 'base' of Hollywood; and on the other hand, an almost exclusively 'industrial' conception of British cinema in terms of monopoly control, government subsidy and the like, with comparatively little attention paid to *auteurs*. Leaving aside the continued presence of a recognisably Griersonian discourse in British film criticism, the British cinema is constituted as a cinema of producers and production finance. If this seems too sweeping, consider that the only major studies of British cinema to be published within the last five years are two on Ealing Studios, one centring on Hammer and a biography of Alexander Korda.[5]

2

All of these studies raise more or less explicit questions about the notion of 'cultural tradition' in Britain. For instance, David Pirie prefaces his survey of the British horror genre and industry with an essay on English Gothic literature; and he argues that the distinctive features of that literature (sado-masochistic themes, possession, vampirism and the like) are almost precisely recapitulated in Hammer horror movies and, once again, recognised abroad as distinctively British. What is now needed, I believe, is a more ambitious mapping of the cultural matrix within which Powell and Pressburger's work is located. Obviously it will not be sufficient merely to juxtapose their oeuvre as a 'literature' against received views of British literature and visual art. These available critical positions must be considered as suspect as the moralistic, 'realist' aesthetic of most film criticism in this country. But as a pointer towards more fruitful directions, I would cite Borges' interlaced essays on Stevenson, Kipling, Chesterton, Wells and Shaw (in *Other Inquisitions*), which develop a potentially subversive critique of the British 'realist hegemony'. Similarly, new approaches to such problematic artists as Blake and Hogarth — not to mention more recent 'literary' artists — may lead to a reconsideration of the specifics and dynamics of cultural formation in Britain.

It is in this context that the present book has been compiled. None of the texts assembled here is offered primarily as exemplary of the critical or theoretical tradition from which it emerges, although the contents of *Criticism* do trace a characteristic set of oppositions and discourses at play in the discussion of British cinema. The overall project is to provide a network of analyses and documents which intersect and serve to define the terrain known as 'Powell and Pressburger' — familiar, though scarcely explored beyond the topographies of 'taste' and 'originality'. Running through these discourses there is a double movement, toward a specificity about the object(s) of study, and also toward an opening onto the wider field of discourses — political, economic, institutional — within which the objects are constituted. The modes of signification discoverable within the films of Powell and Pressburger need to be examined in relation to current work on general signifying practices. And in an area fraught with often ill-considered moral and aesthetic judgment, the constitution of the Powell/ Pressburger 'texts' needs to be grasped in its concrete historical circumstances.

NOTES
1 Peter Wollen, *Signs and Meaning in the Cinema* (London 1972) 1972 Conclusion. p.167. My italics.
2 *loc cit*, p.168.
3 Stephen Heath, 'Comment on "The Idea of Authorship"', *Screen* vol 14 n 3, Autumn 1973 p.88.
4 Roland Barthes, 'The Death of the Author', *Image-Music-Text* (New York 1977)
5 Charles Barr, *Ealing Studios* (London 1977). Also Barr's two part article on Ealing in *Screen*); John Ellis, 'Made in Ealing', *Screen* vol 16 no 1, Spring 1975; David Pirie, *A Heritage of Horror* (London 1973); Karol Kulik, *Alexander Korda* (London 1975).

1   Chronicle

Ian Christie

This *Chronicle* is a combination of filmography, bibliography, biography and memoir. It lists, in chronological order, all the films with which Michael Powell and Emeric Pressburger have been associated, all the important books and articles about their work, and the main events of their careers as filmmakers. Selective information is included on the work of their regular collaborators, together with a running commentary on developments in the British film industry. The result is not intended as a *history*, but rather an outline of 'the field of possibilities, the form of operations, the types of transformations' (Michel Foucault). By introducing material not obviously 'relevant' to the work of Powell and Pressburger, it is hoped to suggest different terms of analysis — to present a series of threads running in a pattern through the fabric of the cinema industry, but inextricably woven together with other threads to form a series of other possible patterns. If there is a strong disposition to read this *Chronicle* as a 'lives and works' narrative, this is perhaps inevitable in view of the limited range of 'reading' models available. But such a mode of presentation should also make it possible to trace different relations of figure to ground, different configurations in that province of North Atlantic cinema which is known as the British film industry.

Certain conventions have been adopted. Full credits are given only in the case of films directed by either Michael Powell or Emeric Pressburger. Films are assigned to the year of their release, and generally listed in the order in which they were trade shown, when these dates are known. (The 'trade show' in Britain is the legally required screening for Board of Trade registration purposes: it provides a convenient indication of the formal date of completion. It should also be noted that the 'release' is not necessarily the first public screening, which is usually the 'premiere run'). No prints are known to exist by the British Film Institute of those films marked with an asterisk(*); although this does not mean, of course, that they are definitively lost. An indication of narrative content has been given in the case of all 'missing' and some rarely-seen films. Since most of these synopses are from journalistic or publicity sources, they should not be regarded as authoritative. Remarks by Powell and Pressburger, unless otherwise attributed, are from interviews by Gough-Yates (1971), or Collins and Christie (1972).

Credit abbreviations are as follows:

d—director. *p.c*—production company. *p*—producer. *exec. p*—executive producer. *assoc. p*—associate producer. *p. sup*—production supervisor. *p. manager*—production manager. *sc*—screenplay. *adapt*—adaptation. *dial*—dialogue. *addit. dial*—additional dialogue. *ph*—photography. *addit. ph*—additional photography. *cam. op*—camera operator. *sp. ph effects*—special photographic effects. *sup. ed*—supervising editor. *ed*—editor. *asst. ed*—assistant editor. *p. designer*—production designer. *sup. a.d*—supervising art director. *a.d*—art director. *asst. a.d*—assistant art director. *set dec*—set decoration. *m*—music. *m.d*—music director. *sd*—sound. *sd rec*—sound recordist. *cost*—costumes. *choreo*—choreography. *asst. d*—assistant director. *t.s*—trade show. *rel*—release. *GB/US dist*—British/American distributor (original). NFA — National Film Archive (BFI).

Note: the longest running time available is given in all cases, although this may not correspond to any actual release version. Many of Powell's films were substantially shortened for re-release, and it is the cut versions that are still distributed. The indications of prizes and awards are not complete.

1902 Emeric Pressburger born in Miskolc, Northern Hungary. His early interests were in mathematics and music and, while still at school, he began to play the violin in amateur orchestras. He left Hungary to study civil engineering at Prague University and later at Stuttgart. His father's death forced him to abandon his studies and, since Miskolc was in the part of Hungary then occupied by Rumania, he decided to stay in Germany. It was there that his first name, Imre, became Emmerich, then Emeric in France and Britain.

1905 Michael Powell born in Bekesbourne, near Canterbury, Kent, the son of an hotelier. He was educated at King's School, Canterbury and Dulwich College; and although determined to enter the cinema, he went to work for the National Provincial Bank in 1922.

1925 Through his father, who owned an hotel at Cap Ferrat near Monte Carlo, Michael Powell is introduced to Harry Lachman, a member of Rex Ingram's film unit. Ingram (1893-1950), an Irish-born actor, director and later sculptor, had become the most important director at Metro after his great success with *The Four Horsemen of the Apocalypse* (1921), which introduced Valentino and restored the ailing company's fortunes. However he was disappointed not to be assigned *Ben-Hur* and, after the arrival of Louis B Mayer to form Metro-Goldwyn-Mayer, he left Hollywood to make *The Arab* on location in North Africa, and was never to return as a director. While finishing the film in France, Ingram discovered the Ciné Studios (later known as the Victorine) outside Nice, which he adopted as a base for

preparation of a second major Blasco Ibanez adaptation, *Mare Nostrum.*
Powell: 'I worked all through. It was a great film to come in on because,
being a spectacular film, full of enormous tricks with a great theme and an
international cast, it gave you ideas which stayed with you all through your
life. Ingram had an epic style. He also had the grand manner . . . My first job
was really to stick around — that was how Harry Lachman put it. Then I
was a grip, but I was unofficially attached to Lachman as the strange,
cultured young Englishman who had a remarkable gift for falling over
things.'

Michael Powell stays with the Ingram unit in Nice and has a small comedy
part written for him in their next production, a Gothic fantasy based on the
fictionalised exploits of 'The Great Beast', Aleister Crowley. *The Magician,*
directed, produced and scripted by Ingram, was based on the novel by
Somerset Maugham. Powell also provides 'comic relief' in *The Garden of
Allah* (1927), which was to be Ingram's last film for MGM.

1927 By 1926 only 5% of films shown in Britain are British-made: in an effort to
halt the drastic decline of indigenous production, the Government
reluctantly takes steps to remedy what are believed to be the causes. The
Cinematograph Films Act is designed to 'restrict blind booking and
advance booking of cinematograph films, and to secure the renting and
exhibition of a certain proportion of British films.' The Act's quotas were
due to come into force in 1928-9.

After *The Garden of Allah,* Powell signs a two-year contract with Harry
Lachman to appear in a projected series of short films (*Travelaughs*) to be
made around Europe. Lachman (1886-1975), an American painter, had
lived in Paris since 1911; after working with Ingram, he stayed in films for
another thirty years as a director (notably of *Dante's Inferno* in 1936), before
returning to painting. However, Powell recalls: 'Talkies were coming in and
our deal with America was off. My two-year contract lasted six months . . .
We closed up the studio, said goodbye to the sun and headed for the fogbelt.
It was January and there was a deep fall of snow in England.'

1928 Lachman goes to British International at Elstree as technical supervisor,
where he directs *Weekend Wives,* and helps Powell to find work also at
Elstree — stills photographer on Hitchcock's *Champagne* and re-cutting
Lupu Pick's *A Knight in London.*

In Berlin, after a period of extreme poverty, Emeric Pressburger sells his
first short stories to Berlin newspapers and begins to send film synopses to
the story department of the largest German film company, Ufa.

1929 The Cinematograph Films Act establishes a renters' quota of 7½% and an
exhibitors' quota of 5% for the first year (the difference intended to ensure
that exhibitors had a 'choice' from the product offered by distributors),

which is to rise by annual increments to a 20% quota for both sectors of the industry by 1936-8. But since the Act makes no reference to levels of finance or quality, its immediate effect is to encourage the production of short, cheaply-made films which nominally satisfied the quota requirements. These 'quota quickies' could be shown as second features with American films — or indeed before the audience arrived! Quota films are either commissioned from small independent producers at absurdly low prices (usually a flat £1 per foot), or produced by the major American companies through British subsidiaries, to utilise 'frozen' revenue. The achievement of the Act is to stimulate, not competitive British production, but an undergrowth of poverty-stricken parochialism.

Powell finishes his spell at Elstree by working (uncredited) on the script of what was to be the first full-length British talkie, Hitchcock's *Blackmail*. According to Frank Launder, Lachman's *Under the Greenwood Tree* could have claimed that honour 'had Harry Lachman got a move on' — it was trade-shown four months later. (*Launder and Gilliat*, Geoff Brown, BFI 1977).

Pressburger sells an original outline to Robert Siodmak, who had made his first feature, *Menschen am Sonntag*, earlier in the year with Edgar G Ulmer and Billy Wilder. As a result, he is taken on by Ufa as a contract writer and assigned an experienced scenarist to collaborate on the full script of *Abschied*.

1930 **Abschied** (Farewell)

d—Robert Siodmak. *p.c*—Ufa. *s.c*—Emeric Pressburger, Irmgard von Cube. *ph*—Eugen Schüfftan.

Pressburger collaborates with Erich Kastner on an adaptation of the latter's short story for a featurette, which was to be Max Ophuls' first film.

Dann Schon Lieber Lebertran* (I'd rather have cod liver oil)

d—Max Ophuls. *p.c*—Ufa. *sc*—Emeric Pressburger, Erich Kästner, Max Ophuls. Based on a story by Kästner.

'It's about some children who, each evening, swallow their cod liver oil and say their prayers before going to sleep. One evening when the room is quite dark, the youngest makes a rather daring prayer: he asks why it's always children who must obey their parents; wouldn't it be possible, once a year, to reverse the roles? The prayer goes up to heaven: God is out, but St Peter is there, just about to fall asleep, and he asks himself why he, too, shouldn't grant a prayer. He goes into a machine room full of complicated instruments and exchanges the cards marked 'parental authority' and 'filial obedience'. The child wakes up with a cigar in his mouth and dressed like a man. He gets up as if everything were normal, goes into his parents' room, wakes them up and sends them off to school.' (Ophuls in an interview from *Cahiers du cinéma*, 1957, reprinted in *Ophuls*, ed Paul Willemen, BFI 1978).

After a spell of unemployment, Powell engaged to write a script for a young American, Jerome Jackson, who is starting to produce for the 'quota' market.

Caste *

d—Campbell Gullan. *p.c*—United Artists/Harry Rowson. *p*—Jerome Jackson. *sc*—Michael Powell, from a play by T W Robertson. *l.p*—Hermione Baddeley, Nora Swinburne, Alan Napier.

A comedy set in 1914. The daughter of a Cockney drunkard marries a young aristocrat, who is presumed killed in action. Powell also works on the production at Walton-on-Thames Studios and remembers the play as 'an old fossil'.

1931 Powell next collaborates on the screenplay of *77 Park Lane,* from a play by Walter Hackett, directed by Albert de Courville. 'By this time Jerry Jackson had got a contract in New York — actually two contracts: one with Fox to do a quota picture of four reels and another with what was then called Ideal Films.'

Two Crowded Hours *

d—Michael Powell *p.c*—Film Engineering. *p*—Jerome Jackson, Henry Cohen. *sc*—J Jefferson Farjeon. *ph*—Geoffrey Faithfull. *ed*—A Seabourne. *a.d*—C Saunders.

John Longden (*Harry Fielding*), Jane Walsh (*Joyce Danton*), Jerry Verno (*Jim*), Michael Hogan (*Scammell*), Edward Barber (*Tom Murray*).

43 mins. *t.s*—8 July. *rel*—28 December. *GB dist*—Fox.

A murderer escapes from prison and tries to kill those who gave evidence against him. The detective gives chase with the help of a taxi driver.
Powell: 'It was played for laughs and thrills and we were payed £1 per foot by Fox, which meant that we got £4000 on delivery, and so we obviously made it for £3000.'

My Friend the King *

d—Michael Powell. *p.c*—Film Engineering. *p*—Jerome Jackson. *sc*—J Jefferson Farjeon, from his own story. *ph*—Geoffrey Faithfull. *ed*—A Seabourne. *a.d*—C Saunders.

Jerry Verno (*Jim*), Robert Holmes (*Captain Felz*), Tracey Holmes (*Count Huelin*), Eric Pavitt (*King Ludwig*), Phyllis Loring (*Princess Helma*), Luli Hohenberg (*Countess Zena*), H Saxon Snell (*Karl*), Victor Fairlie (*Josef*).

47 mins. *t.s*—23 September. *rel*—4 April 1932. *GB dist*—Paramount.

'Jerry Verno, who scored such a decided comedy hit in *Two Crowded Hours* as a taxi driver, continues his automobile career in this feature . . . as a taxi driver who gets involved in a plot to abduct the youthful king of a Ruritanian country.' (*Picturegoer* 13.3.32). Powell: 'It was a very weak story about a little boy who was some foreign king staying in London and got kidnapped. I only remember it as a complete failure.'

Rynox *

d—Michael Powell. p.c—Film Engineering, for Ideal Films. p—Jerome Jackson. sc—Jerome Jackson, Michael Powell and Philip MacDonald, from his novel. ph—Geoffrey Faithfull. ed.—A Seabourne.

Stewart Rome (*Boswell Marsh/F X Benedik*), Dorothy Boyd (*Peter*), John Longden (*Tony Benedik*), Edward Willard (*Captain James*), Charles Paton, Fletcher Lightfoot, Şybil Grove, Leslie Mitchell.

48 mins. t.s—4 November. rel—7 May 1932. GB dist—Ideal.

'This unpretentious mystery picture has some claim to originality in conception and affords Stewart Rome a chance of showing that he is an actor of ability. He appears here in the dual role of a business magnate, Benedik, and a mysterious gentleman, Marsh, who threatens the magnate. In the end Benedik is found murdered. It eventually transpires that he had invented the character of Marsh so that he might disappear and collect the insurance money on his assumed death.' (*Picturegoer* 5.3.32). Powell: 'The other one was for us a super production because we got paid £4500 for it and this was a rather long film, a five reeler . . . Philip MacDonald was the best thriller writer in those days and he still is, as far as I'm concerned, one of the best.'

The Rasp *

d—Michael Powell. p.c—Film Engineering. p—Jerome Jackson. sc—Philip MacDonald, from his own story. ph—Geoffrey Faithfull. a.d—Frank Wells.

Claude Horton (*Anthony Gethryn*), Phyllis Loring (*Lucia Masterson*), C M Hallard (*Sir Arthur Coates*), James Raglan (*Alan Deacon*), Thomas Weguelin (*Inspector Boyd*), Carol Coombe (*Dora Masterson*), Leonard Brett (*Jimmy Masterson*).

44 mins. t.s—3 December. rel—11 April 1932. GB dist—Fox.

An enterprising young newspaper owner discovers a cabinet minister dead when he arrives to interview him: the murder weapon is a rasp. Gethryn starts his own investigation and is able to cast doubt on the police's suspect. He finally succeeds in tricking the murderer into a confession. Powell: '*The Rasp* wasn't a terrific success but it did all right. By this time Philip MacDonald, having seen *Rynox,* became interested in us and volunteered to write two or three original scripts for the little team of Jackson and Powell.'

The Star Reporter *

d—Michael Powell. p.c—Film Engineering. p—Jerome Jackson. sc—Ralph Smart, Philip MacDonald, from a story by MacDonald. ph—Geoffrey Faithfull. add. ph—Michael Powell. a.d—Frank Wells.

Harold French (*Major Starr*), Isla Bevan (*Lady Susan Loman*), Garry Marsh (*Mandel*), Spencer Trevor (*Lord Longbourne*), Anthony Holles (*Bonzo*), Noel Dainton (*Colonel*), Elsa Graves (*Oliver*), Philip Morant (*Jeff*).

44 mins. *t.s*—10 December. *rel*—9 May 1932. *GB dist*—Fox.

'Unpretentious and fantastic story of a smash-and-grab-raid, with a newspaper reporter — in the American tradition — bringing the crooks to justice.' (*Picturegoer* 7.5.32). Powell: 'What staggered Jackson was that there was a scene of meeting someone off an Atlantic liner, so I said to Jerry, "Give me a hand camera." He said, "What for? You realise they're £8 to hire?" I said, "I don't want to haggle. I want to go to Southampton and shoot some stuff of the *Queen Mary*." He let me go and I shot some very good stuff of the liner coming in and docking . . . and they just cut it into the picture. It really only cost £8 plus the film. Then we did the rest of it in the studio.'

Das Ekel (The Scoundrel)

d—Franz Wenzler, Eugen Schufftan. *p.c*—Ufa. *sc*—Emeric Pressburger, from an idea by Reimann and Impekoven. *rel*—2 June.

A comedy of the working day in Berlin.

Der Kleine Seitensprung (The Little Escapade)

d—Reinhold Schünzel. *p.c*—Ufa. *p.sup*—Günther Stapenhorst. *sc*—Emeric Pressburger, Reinhold Schünzel, from an idea by Schünzel. *rel*—14 August. [Also a French version, *Le Petit Ecart*. *co-d.*—Henri Chomette. *dial*—Raoul Ploquin, Henri Chomette.]

A wife believes her husband has been deceiving her and decides to have some fun at his expense. Several imbroglios provoke the lawyer husband to seek a double divorce, on behalf of himself and a hoaxed husband. His wife sorts everything out and the lawyer wins back a much-loved wife whom he almost lost.

Ronny

d—Reinhold Schünzel. *p.c*—Ufa. *p.sup*—Günther Stapenhorst. *sc*—Emeric Pressburger, Reinhold Schünzel. *m*—Emmerich Kalman, arr. Erich Wolfgang Korngold. *rel*—16 December. [Also a French version, with the same title. *d*—Roger Le Bon. *dial*—Raoul Ploquin.]

Ronny, a young designer, is on her way to the capital of a Ruritanian kingdom with the costumes she has created for an operetta written by the prince. On her journey, she meets the prince and takes part in his operetta.

Pressburger was in the production unit headed by Stapenhorst, working closely with a fellow-Hungarian, Reinhold Schünzel. Schünzel (1888-1954) had acted in early films by Lubitsch, Oswald and Jacoby (and played Tiger Brown in Pabst's *Threepenny Opera*), before starting to direct a series of ironic comedies, which included *Amphitryon* (1935). In the United States from 1937, he directed a number of films and his appearances as an actor include *Hangmen also Die* (Lang 1943), *First Comes Courage* (Arzner, 1943), *The Hitler Gang* (Farrow, 1944) and *Notorious* (Hitchcock, 1946).

In this same year, Adolf Wohlbrück (later Anton Walbrook) makes his film debut in E A Dupont's *Salto Mortale,* a circus melodrama. Walbrook (born 1900, Vienna) had studied with Reinhardt and appeared in Vienna, Munich and Dresden with great success. After his film debut, he worked regularly in cinema and theatre: he came to Britain in 1937 after an unsuccessful visit to Hollywood for *Michael Strogoff* (1936).

Salto Mortale was designed by Dupont's regular art director, Alfred Junge, whose film career had started in the early 20s, assisting Paul Leni with the design of such heavily stylised films as *Backstairs* (Jessner, 1921) and *Waxworks* (Leni, 1924). He had accompanied Dupont to Britain for the latter's films at Elstree (*Moulin Rouge, Piccadilly, Two Worlds, Cape Forlorn* 1928-30); and after several more assignments in Germany and France (including Korda's *Marius* at Joinville), the following year he settled in England permanently.

1932 Hotel Splendide *

d—Michael Powell *p.c*—Gaumont-British. *p*—Jerome Jackson. *sc*—Ralph Smart, from a story by Philip MacDonald. *ph*—Geoffrey Faithfull, Arthur Grant. *a.d*—C Saunders.

Jerry Verno (*Jerry Mason*), Anthony Holles (*Mrs Le Grange*), Edgar Norfolk ('*Gentleman Charlie*'), Philip Morant (*Mr Meek*), Sybil Groves (*Mrs Harkness*), Vera Sherbourne (*Joyce Dacre*), Paddy Browne (*Miss Meek*).

53 mins. *t.s*—23 March. *rel*—18 July. *GB dist*—Ideal.

'Jerry Mason inherits the Hotel Splendide at Speymouth, and his disappointment at first sight of it is tempered by his determination to boost it. To the hotel, whose existing guests are an invalid lady, Mrs Le Grange, and her grand-daughter, and a vacuous young couple named Meek, come Gentleman Charlie, a released convict, and his confederate, there to recover the Dysart pearls, which were buried some time previously at the spot where the hotel now stands. Charlie believes erroneously that his rival, 'Pussy' Saunders is in prison . . .' (*Biograph* 30.3.32).

C.O.D. *

d—Michael Powell. *p.c*—Westminster Films. *p*—Jerome Jackson. *sc*—Ralph Smart, from a story by Philip MacDonald. *ph*—Geoffrey Faithfull. *a.d*—Frank Wells.

Garry Marsh (*Peter Craven*), Hope Davey (*Frances*), Arthur Stratton (*Briggs*), Sybil Grove (*Mrs Briggs*), Roland Culver (*Edward*), Peter Gawthorne (*Detective*), Cecil Ramage (*Vyner*), Bruce Belfrage (*Philip*).

66 mins. *t.s*—17 March. *rel*—22 August. *GB dist*—United Artists.

'Peter Craven, temporarily down and out, enters a West End mansion during the absence of the servants and, while helping himself to refreshments, is confronted by a lovely girl, Frances, who offers to pay him to dispose of the body of her stepfather, who has just been murdered in circumstances likely to incriminate her. Peter takes the body in a trunk to the cloakroom at St Pancras, but on his return he and Frances are annoyed to find that the body has been put in its original position in the library. Frances' cousin, Edward, arrived with a friend and sends for the police. While Frances is being cross-examined, Peter calls on a doctor, chloroforms him and, going back to the house in his name, forces a confession at the point of a stethescope from a confederate, who denounces Edward as the murderer. Peter and Edward then fight a revolver duel up to the top of the house, from which Edward falls to his death and Peter returns to arrange a marriage with Frances.' (*Biograph* 23.3.32).

His Lordship[*]

d—Michael Powell. *p.c*—Westminster Films. *p*—Jerome Jackson. *sc*— Ralph Smart. Based on the novel *The Right Honorable* by Oliver Madox Heuffer. *ph*—Geoffrey Faithfull. *a.d*—Frank Wells. *m/lyrics*—V C Clinton-Baddeley, Eric Maschwitz.

Jerry Verno (*Bert Gibbs*), Janet McGrew (*Ilya Myona*), Ben Weldon (*Washington Lincoln*), Polly Ward (*Leninia*), Peter Gawthorne (*Ferguson*), Muriel George (*Mrs Gibbs*), Michael Hogan (*Comrade Curzon*), V C Clinton-Baddeley (*Comrade Howard*), Patric Ludlow (*Hon Grimsthwaite*).

77 mins. *t.s*—2 June. *rel*—5 December. *GB dist*—United Artists.

'Jerry Verno, that clever and versatile British comedian, is very badly served with material in this queer mixture of musical comedy, burlesque and satire.' (*Picturegoer* 3.12.32).

Born Lucky [*]

d—Michael Powell. *p.c*—Westminster Films. *p*—Jerome Jackson. *sc*— Ralph Smart. Based on the novel *Mops* by Oliver Sandys. *a.d*—Ian Campbell-Gray.

Talbot O'Farrell (*Turnips*), Renee Ray (*Mops*), John Longden (*Frank Dale*), Ben Welden (*Harriman*), Helen Ferrers (*Lady Chard*), Barbara Gott (*Cook*), Paddy Browne (*Patty*), Roland Gillett (*John Chard*).

78 mins. *t.s*—5 December. *rel*—6 April 1933. *GB dist*—MGM.

'Simple story of a humble girl's rise to stage fame . . . Servants' hall humour, music and songs are included.' (*Picturegoer* 1.4.33).

Das Schöne Abenteur (The Happy Adventure)

d—Reinhold Schünzel. *p.c*—Ufa. *p.sup*—Günther Stapenhorst. *sc*— Emeric Pressburger, Reinhold Schünzel. Based on a play by Robert de Fiers, Gaston Armand de Caillavet, Etienne Rey. [Also French version, *La Belle Aventure*. *d*—Roger Le Bon. *dial*—Etienne Rey].

Helen has agreed to marry a man with whom she is not in love, but on the day of the wedding her cousin comes in time for them to elope together. They go to stay with her grandmother, who takes the young man to be the husband and insists that they share a room. The official fiancé gladly gives way to a love match.

Sehnsucht 202 (Yearning 202)

d—Max Neufeld. *p.c*—Deutsch-Oesterreichische (Germany/Austria). *p*—Karl Erlich. *sc*—Emeric Pressburger, Irmgard von Cube, Karl Farkas. [Also French version, *Désir 22.* or *Une Jeune Fille et un Million. d*—Fred Ellis. *sc*—Fred Ellis, Serge Veber]

A musical comedy set in Vienna (the title refers to the name of a perfume). Two young women reply to newspaper advertisements, but by mistake their replies are confused. Meanwhile two young directors of a perfume company, who initially have different intentions towards them, eventually propose marriage.

Alexander Korda, who was to become an influential and flamboyant force in British film production, arrives in England at the end of 1931. Within six months he has fulfilled his immediate contract with Paramount British and set up London Film Productions in partnership with his brothers Zoltan (director) and Vincent (painter and designer), and representatives of British financial interests. Korda (born 1893 in Túrkeve, Hungary) had already launched several film careers in various countries. He first became a successful journalist, director and studio owner in Budapest, until the Rumanian occupation of 1919 forced him to flee; next came a spell in Vienna, which culminated in the £500,000 production of *Samson and Delilah* (1923); then Berlin, where he directed another six films, the last for Fox's German subsidiary (a quota system in Germany predated that in Britain); from Berlin he went to Hollywood in 1927 and made ten relatively undistinguished films in the next four years. On his return to Europe in 1931, Korda found work in Paris making German and French versions of American films for Paramount's French 'quota' subsidiary. After a Pagnol adaptation, *Marius*, he accepted an invitation from Paramount to try to improve the standard of their British quota product. The first result was a re-make of Harry d'Arrast's *Service for Ladies*, for which Leslie Howard was brought back from Hollywood and Junge acted as art director.

1933 . . . und es leuchtet die Pussta (. . and the Plains are Gleaming)

d—Heinz Hille. *p.c*—Ufa/Hunnia-Film (Budapest). *sc*—Emeric Pressburger. Based on the novel *The Old Crook* by Koloman Mikszath.

A country comedy set in Hungary.

Une Femme au Volant (A Woman at the Wheel)

d—Kurt Gerron, Pierre Billon. *p.c*—Films RP (France). *p*—Romain Pines. *sc*—Emeric Pressburger. *dial*—Jacques Natanson.

A young sportsman, the heir to a tyre manufacturing business, wants to end the rivalry which exists between his father's company and its main competitor, by marrying the daughter of the rival family.

In April, the Association of Cinematograph Technicians becomes the first trade union in Britain to organise film production workers. This was the outcome of various mounting pressures. The low profitability of 'quota' production often forced technicians to accept low wages and long hours. Another factor was the growing tendency among American companies to bring over Hollywood technicians for senior posts in their British subsidiaries, while ambitious British companies (like Korda's newly-formed London Films) employed a high proportion of European staff, thus denying British technicians both full employment and reasonable chance of promotion. 'At the beginning of 1933, while Korda employed Périnal (French director of photography) plus an American editor and an American trickwork expert, an American cameraman headed Ealing studios, and Gaumont-British were shooting *Rome Express* with an American and a German star, an Austrian cinematographer and an American editor. It was there, at the G-B Shepherd's Bush Studios, that the first move was made towards the establishment of the ACT'. (Michael Chanan, *Labour Power in the British Film Industry*, BFI 1976). Despite the incentive to seek better conditions and prospects, it was not until 1935 that the ACT became effectively organised and, in 1936 negotiated its first overall agreement with a studio.

The Fire Raisers *

d—Michael Powell. *p.c*—Gaumont-British. *p*—Jerome Jackson. *sc*—Powell, Jerome Jackson, from an original story. *ph*—Leslie Rowson. *ed*—D N Twist. *a.d*—Alfred Junge. *cost*—Cordon Conway. *sd*—A F Birch.

Leslie Banks (*Jim Bronson*), Anne Grey (*Arden Brent*), Carol Goodner (*Helen Vaughan*), Frank Cellier (*Brent*), Francis L Sullivan (*Stedding*), Laurence Anderson (*Twist*), Harry Caine (*Bates*), Joyce Kirby (*Polly*), George Merritt (*Sonners*).

77 mins *t.s*—18 September. *rel*—22 January 1934. *GB dist*—Woolf & Freedman.

'Bronson, a fire assessor, builds up a big business by unscrupulous methods and marries the daughter of an eminent underwriter at Lloyds, against her father's wishes. His extravagances on the turf, however, eventually cause him to join up with the fire-raiser. When Bronson is unmasked he deliberately goes to his own death after saving the life of an investigator engaged to his typist; his spectacular end saving his wife and her father from disgrace.' (*Picturegoer* 20.1.34). Powell: 'We moved into what you might describe as a sort of Warner Brothers newspaper headline story. As we'd made our mark with these little quota pictures, Jerry landed a contract with Mick Balcon to do four films. We were, except for one script they handed us, to supply the subjects and write our own scripts . . . We went straight on to do the one we had written ourselves, which was based on a newspaper case at that time about a fire assessor for an insurance company who started his own fires.'

The commercial success in Britain and America of *The Private Life of Henry VIII* establishes Korda's reputation and restores the belief that 'British' films can compete in world markets.

1934 The Night of the Party *

d—Michael Powell. p.c—Gaumont-British. p—Jerome Jackson. sc—Roland Pertwee, John Hastings Turner, from their own play. ph—Glen MacWilliams. sup. a.d—Alfred Junge.

Leslie Banks (*Sir John Holland*), Ian Hunter (*Guy Kennington*), Jane Baxter (*Peggy Studholme*), Ernest Thesiger (*Chiddiatt*), Viola Keats (*John Holland*), Malcolm Keen (*Lord Studholme*), Jane Millican (*Anna Chiddiatt*), Muriel Akad (*Princess*), John Turnbull (*Ramage*), Laurence Anderson (*Defence Counsel*), W Graham Brown (*General Piddington*).

61 mins. t.s—1 Feb. GB rel—16 July. GB dist—Gaumont-British. US rel—floating 1935/6. US title — *The Murder Party*.

'Lord Studholme, a ruthless newspaper magnate, generally feared, gives a dinner party in honour of a foreign princess. After dinner, a game called "Murder" is suggested, and when the lights, which had been lowered, are turned up it is discovered that Studholme has actually been murdered. Suspicion is directed towards Sir John Holland, Commissioner of Police, whose daughter, Joan, Studholme had attempted to seduce; Joan herself; Guy Kennion, Studholme's secretary, who had secretly married his daughter, Peggy; General Piddington, Studholme's father-in-law; and Chiddiatt, an ultra-modern novelist, whose works Studholme had ridiculed. Guy is ultimately arrested, but during his trial at the Old Bailey, Chiddiatt, whose mind becomes unhinged, spectacularly confesses, and then kills himself.' (*Kine Weekly* 8.2.34). Powell: 'Everybody hated it but it was a terrific cast . . . it was one of those Agatha Christie stories where everybody's a character and it ends up with an Old Bailey court case. I was bored to death with it but I did the best I could. After *The Fire Raisers*, we went back to *The Night of the Party* and did three days extra re-takes, which made a little more sense of it, but I've never seen it again.'

Red Ensign

d—Michael Powell p.c—Gaumont British. p—Jerome Jackson. sc—Powell, Jerome Jackson. addit. dial—L du Garde Peach. ph—Leslie Rowson. sup. a.d—Alfred Junge.

Leslie Banks (*David Barr*), Carol Goodner (*June MacKinnon*), Frank Vosper (*Lord Dean*), Alfred Drayton (*Manning*), Donald Calthorp (*MacLeod*), Allan Jeayes (*Emerson*), Campbell Gullan (*Hannay*), Percy Parsons (*Casey*), Fewlass Llewllyn (*Sir Gregory*), Henry Oscar (*Raglan*).

69 mins. t.s—2 February. GB rel—4 June. GB dist—Gaumont-British. US rel—floating 1935/6. US title — *Strike!* Preserved in NFA.

Barr, the managing director of a shipbuilding company on Clydeside, anticipates a revival in shipping and risks everything to develop a new design. While his fellow directors refuse to back him, a rival attempts sabotage. The only woman on the board offers money, against the wishes of her fiancé. Barr forges the latter's signature and is arrested, but his gamble pays off and the new ship succeeds. Powell recalls that this was also based on topical events and had some exteriors shot in Glasgow.

Something Always Happens

d—Michael Powell. *p.c*—Warner Brothers-First National. *exec p*—Irving Asher. *sc*—Brock Williams. *ph*—Basil Emmott. *a.d*—Peter Proud. *ed*—Bert Bates.

Ian Hunter (*Peter Middleton*), Nancy O'Neil (*Cynthia Hatch*), John Singer (*Billy*), Peter Gawthorne (*Mr Hatch*), Muriel George (*Mrs Badger*), Barry Livesey (*George Hamlin*), Millicent Wolf (*Glenda*), Louie Emery (*Mrs Tremlett*), Reg Marcus ('*Coster*').

69 mins. *t.s*—21 June. *rel*—10 December. *GB dist*—Warner Brothers-First National. Preserved in NFA.

'Peter Middleton, a resourceful young motor salesman down on his luck, has the good fortune to meet and fall in love with Cynthia, daughter of the business magnate Hatch, and she, without disclosing her identity, introduces him to her father. When his scheme to put Hatch's chain of petrol stations on its feet is turned down, he takes the latter's advice and sells it, and himself, to a rival concern.' (*Kine Weekly* 28.6.34). Powell: 'We played it all out for laughs; great speed, excellent dialogue and it was about a chap who never paid for anything.'

Korda visits Hollywood and becomes an owner-member of United Artists, thus securing an American outlet for London Productions.

The Girl in the Crowd *

d—Michael Powell. *p.c*—First National. *exec. p*—Irving Asher. *sc*—Brock Williams. *ph*—Basil Emmott. *ed*—Bert Bates.

Barry Clifton (*David Gordon*), Patricia Hilliard (*Marian*), Googie Withers (*Sally*), Harold French (*Bob*), Clarence Blakiston (*Mr Peabody*), Margaret Gunn (*Joyce*), Richard Littledale (*Bill Manners*), Phyllis Morris (*Mrs Lewis*), Patric Knowles (*Tom Burrows*), Marjorie Corbett (*Secretary*), Brenda Lawless (*Policewoman*), Barbara Waring (*Mannequin*), Eve Lister (*Ruby*), Betty Lyne (*Phyllis*), Melita Bell (*Assistant Manageress*), John Wood (*Harry*).

52 mins. *t.s*—4 December. *rel*—20 May 1935. *GB dist*— First National.

'David Gordon, a bookseller patronised by a co-ed college, marries one of the students, Marian. They keep in touch with the 'old gang' and Marian, who has never met her husband's best friend Bob, gives him some advice on the phone about securing a wife — in brief, that he should follow the first girl that attracts him. Unfortunately, this happens to be Marian, and subsequent events land Bob in court for insulting behaviour; further complications land David, Marian and 'the gang' there too. Eventually everything is straightened out with the help of two of the new school of policemen who had been schoolmates of Bob.' (*Kine Weekly* 6.12.34). Powell: 'It was a complete failure, nobody ever saw it. This was something somebody got out of the drawer and Irving Asher said, "For God's sake, shoot this." It was Googie Withers' first chance.'

Joseph Arthur Rank commissions his first short religious film, *Mastership*, from an ex-advertising man Aveling Ginever for £2700. J Arthur (born 1888) was the youngest son of the milling millionaire Joseph Rank and, like his father, a devout Methodist. While working in the family firm, he felt a call to evangelise through film and began to equip Methodist churches with projectors bought from Gaumont-British. After *Mastership*, he persuaded G-B to make three religious films; then, through John Corfield, an independent producer who made a further two evangelical shorts for him, Rank was introduced to Lady Yule, an eccentric and wealthy widow, and in October they formed British National Films. Their first production was *Turn of the Tide*, a story of rivalry between two Yorkshire fishing families, largely shot on location at Robin Hood's Bay, near Whitby.

1935 Monsieur Sans-Gêne

d—Karl Anton. *p.c*—Amora Film (France). *p*—M Strausz. *sc*—Emeric Pressburger, René Pujol.

Fernand thinks he is kissing his friend in the cinema, but it is a stranger sitting next to him. When he sees that she is charming, despite being free with her hands, he does not dare admit his mistake, which eventually leads to marriage. [Re-made in the United States as *One Rainy Afternoon* (1936). *d*—Rowland V Lee. With Francis Lederer, Ida Lupino.]

La Vie Parisienne

d—Robert Siodmak. *p.c*—Néro-Film (France). *sc*—Emeric Pressburger, Benno Vigny, Michel Carre. *m*—Jacques Offenbach, *arr*—Maurice Jaubert. [Also English version, *Parisienne Life*.]

A rich Brazilian Mendoza visited Paris in 1900 and was romantically involved with the star of Offenbach's *La Vie Parisienne*, which was playing at that time. Thirty-five years later, he returns with his son and granddaughter, who is engaged to a young Frenchman. But Mendoza's puritannical son forbids the marriage. Mendoza's and the actress's friends conspire to change his mind and soon succeed in converting him to 'Parisian life'.

In September, Emeric Pressburger comes to England with a stateless passport.

Korda secures the backing of the Prudential Insurance Company for London Film Productions, the first major City investment in British production. An initial payment of £250,000 enables him to lease Isleworth Studios and he announces a £2 million production programme.

British National's *Turn of the Tide* wins a prize at the Venice Festival but is snubbed by British distributors, despite an advance distribution guarantee from Gaumont-British. C M Woolf, now managing director of G-B, resigns in May and starts General Film Distributors (GFD). Rank becomes a director of General Cinema Finance Corporation, which buys up GFD; he also joins the board of a new studio complex under construction at Pinewood.

Lazybones

d—Michael Powell, *p.c*—Real Art. *exec. p*—Julius Hagen. *sc*—Gerald Fairlie, from a play by Ernest Denny. *ph*—Arthur Crabtree. *sup. ed*—Frank Harris.

Claire Luce (*Kitty McCarthy*), Ian Hunter (*Sir Reginald Ford*), Sara Allgood (*Bridget*), Bernard Nedell (*Mike McCarthy*), Michael Shepley (*Hildebrand Pope*), Bobbie Comber (*Kemp*), Denys Blakelock (*Hugh Ford*), Marjorie Gaskell (*Marjory Ford*), Pamela Carne (*Lottie Pope*), Harold Warrender (*Lord Melton*), Miles Malleson (*Pessimist*), Fred Withers (*Richards*), Frank Morgan (*Tom*), Fewlass Llewllyn (*Lord Brockley*), Paul Blake (*Viscount Woodland*).

65 mins. *t.s*—17 Jan. *rel*—24 June. *GB dist*—RKO. Preserved in NFA.

'A comedy of impoverished aristocracy endeavouring to retrieve the family fortune by marrying the lazy eldest son to an American heiress.' (*MFB*). Powell: '*Lazybones* was a film I made at Twickenham in the days when Julius Hagen was the Czar of Twickenham and he had such marvellous contracts to supply these cheap films, that he had the studio working twenty-four hours day and night. This film was made with two West End actors who only came down after the show at night, and we shot all night making a comedy. Can you imagine? *Lazybones* was about a man who couldn't get up in the morning.'

The Love Test *

d—Michael Powell. *p.c*—Leslie Landau for Fox British. *p.*—Leslie Landau. *sc*—Selwyn Jepson. Based on a story by Jack Celestin. *ph*—Arthur Crabtree.

Judy Gunn (*Mary*), Louis Hayward (*John*), Dave Hucheson (*Thompson*), Googie Withers (*Minnie*), Morris Harvey (*President*), Aubrey Dexter (*Vice-President*), Eve Turner (*Kathleen*), Bernard Miles (*Allan*), Jack Knight (*Managing Director*), Gilbert Davis (*Chief Chemist*), Shayle Gardner (*Night Watchman*), James Craig (*Boiler Man*).

63 mins. *t.s*—2 December 1934. *rel*—1 July. *GB dist*—Fox British.

'Thompson, chief laboratory assistant to a chemical firm, is afraid of being beaten in the race for promotion by Mary, a studious girl, and plans with his colleagues to wreck her chances of promotion by distracting her with thoughts of love. John, another employee, is selected to act the role of Romeo, but the scheme misfires when he falls in love with Mary and she with him. Mary is promoted and the jealous Thompson, not to be outdone, first creates misunderstanding between Mary and John, and then goes so far as to steal a valuable formula invented by John. He is, however, found out in time and happiness at last comes the way of the young lovers.' (*Kine Weekly* 10.1.35).

The Phantom Light

d—Michael Powell. *p.c*—Gaumont British. *p*—Jerome Jackson. *sc*—Ralph Smart. Based on a play by Evadne Price, Joan Roy Byford. *addit. dial*—J Jefferson Farjeon, Austin Melford. *ph*—Roy Kellino. *ed*—Derek Twist. *a.d*—Alex Vetchinsky. *m*—Louis Levy.

Binnie Hale (*Alice Bright*), Gordon Harker (*Sam Higgins*), Ian Hunter (*Jim Pierce*), Donald Calthrop (*David Owen*), Milton Rosmer (*Dr Carey*), Reginald Tate (*Tom Evans*), Mickey Brantford (*Bob Peters*), Herbert Lomas (*Claff Owen*), Fewlass Llewllyn (*Griffith Owen*), Alice O'Day (*Mrs Owen*), Barry O'Neill (*Captain Pierce*), Edgar K Bruce (*Sergeant Owen*), Louie Emery (*Station Mistress*).

76 mins. *t.s*—9 January. *rel*—5 August. *GB dist*—Gaumont-British. [Re-issued 1950] Preserved in NFA.

A new keeper arrives at a lighthouse off the Welsh coast where there has been a series of unexplained occurences. He is joined by a naval lieutenant and a lady detective (both incognito), who reveal a wreckers' plot to black out the lighthouse and lure ships ashore. Powell: 'I had to take this very stagey play and somehow turn it into a very atmospheric melodrama, which looked as though it was all shot on location — Portmadoc.'

The Price of a Song *

d—Michael Powell. *p.c*—Fox British. *sc*—Anthony Gittens.

Campbell Gullan (*Arnold Grierson*), Marjorie Corbett (*Margaret Nevern*), Gerald Fielding (*Michael Hardwicke*), Dora Barton (*Letty Grierson*), Charles Mortimer (*Oliver Broom*), Oriel Ross (*Elsie*), Henry Caine (*Stringer*), Sybil Grove (*Mrs Bancroft*), Eric Maturin (*Nevern*), Felix Aylmer (*Graham*), Cynthia Stock (*Mrs Bush*), Mavis Clair (*Maudie Bancroft*).

67 mins. *t.s*—24 May. *rel*—7 October. *GB dist*—Fox British.

'Arnold Grierson, a bookmaker's clerk, finds himself in financial difficulties and forces his stepdaughter to marry Nevern, a caddish song-writer, for his money. When she finally finds life unbearable with Nevern, and decides to divorce him and marry Hardwicke, a newspaper reporter, Grierson schemes to murder Nevern in the hope that Margaret will inherit his money. After secretly building up alibi upon alibi, he perpetrates what he believes to be the perfect crime, only to allow an incredible slip to prove his undoing.' (*Kine Weekly* 30.5.35).

Someday *

d—Michael Powell. *p.c*—Warner British. *p*—Irving Asher. *sc*—Brock Williams. Based on the novel *Young Nowheres* by I A R Wylie. *ph*—Basil Emmott, Monty Berman. *ed*—Bert Bates. *a.d*—Ian Campbell-Gray.

Esmond Knight (*Curley Blake*), Margaret Lockwood (*Emily*), Henry Mollison (*Canley*), Sunday Wilshin (*Betty*), Raymond Lovell (*Carr*), Ivor Bernard (*Hope*), George Pughe (*Milkman*), Jane Cornell (*Nurse*).

68 mins. *t.s*—17 July. *rel*—18 November. *GB dist*—Warner Brothers-First National.

'Curley is a lift-boy in a block of flats, in love with Emily who "does" for Mr Canley, one of the tenants, but their wages are so low that marriage seems to be impossible. Curley plans a surprise supper for Emily on her return from hospital, in the flat of a tenant, Mr Carr, who is supposed to be abroad; but he interrupts them and there is a fight. Curley is charged with illegal entry and assault by Mr Carr but everything ends happily.' (*Monthly Film Bulletin* 18).

Hein Heckroth (1901-1970), German painter and stage designer, invited to London to design the Kurt Weill opera *A Kingdom for a Cow*. He had made his reputation with the decor for Kurt Joos's ballet *The Green Table* (1932), but had been designing for ballet and opera since 1924. He continued to work in Britain, at Glyndebourne, the Old Vic, Birmingham Repertory Theatre and for the New Russian Ballet; he was based for a time at Dartington Hall.

La Cucaracha (Lloyd Corrigan) and *Becky Sharp* (Mamoulian) are the first full-length films to be released in three-colour subtractive Technicolor, which then becomes the standard colour process until the introduction of Eastmancolor in 1952. Natalie and Herbert Kalmus had been experimenting with colour processes since 1915 and a two-colour subtractive system was used from 1922 for sequences in otherwise monochrome films. Natalie Kalmus insisted on keeping close control over the use of colour in all early Technicolor films.

1936 Her Last Affaire [*]

d—Michael Powell. *p.c*—New Ideal. *p*—Simon Rowson, Geoffrey Rowson. *sc*—Ian Dalrymple. Based on the play *S.O.S.* by Walter Ellis. *ph*—Geoffrey Faithfull. *sd*—George Burgess.

Hugh Williams (*Alan Heriot*), Viola Keats (*Lady Avril Weyre*), Francis L Sullivan (*Sir Julian Weyre*), Sophie Stewart (*Judy Weyre*), Felix Aylmer (*Lord Carnforth*), Cecil Parker (*Sir Arthur Harding*), John Gardner (*Boxall*), Henry Caine (*Inspector Marsh*), Gerrard Tyrell (*Martin*).

78 mins. *t.s*—21 October 1925. *rel*—25 May. *GB dist*—Producers Distributing Corporation.

'Alan Heriot, secretary to Sir Julian Weyre, an ambitious politician, wishes to marry Weyre's daughter Judy, but is prevented because his father had died under a cloud. Having reason to believe that Weyre's wife Avril can clear his father, he makes love to her and induces her to spend a night with him at a country inn. Once in their room, Alan lays his cards on the table and Avril writes a confession clearing his father, but when he refuses to stay with her, she throws the missive away. Following this, she dies from a heart attack, and her death coincides with a wireless SOS to the effect that her medicine has been wrongly dispensed and contains poison. Panic overtakes Alan and he absconds, but after prolonged investigation Avril's confession is discovered, scandal avoided and his romance with Judy re-established.'

(*Kine Weekly* 24.10.35). Powell: '*Her Last Affaire* was a play which had a great success because it was the first legitimate part played by Gracie Fields and funnily enough it was a straight melodrama . . . It was made at the old Beaconsfield Studios, but I don't remember it being a very happy picture: Hugh Williams was back from Hollywood at that time — he was an extremely polished,arrogant young actor — and I enjoyed working with him on it. I think it was the first script Ian Dalrymple wrote. The actual drama was a bit too stagey to make it a success.'

The Brown Wallet[*]

d—Michael Powell. *p.c*—Warner Brothers-First National. *exec. p*—Irving Asher. *sc*—Ian Dalrymple, from a story by Stacy Aumonier. *ph*—Basil Emmott.

Patric Knowles (*John Gillespie*), Nancy O'Neill (*Eleanor*), Henry Caine (*Simmonds*), Henrietta Watson (*Aunt Mary*), Charlotte Leigh (*Miss Barton*), Shayle Gardner (*Wotherspoone*), Edward Dalby (*Minting*), Eliot Makeham (*Hobday*), Bruce Winston (*Julian Thorpe*), Jane Millican (*Miss Bloxham*), Louis Goodrich (*Coroner*), Dick Francis, George Mills (*Detectives*).

68 mins. *t.s*—25 February. *rel*—20 July. *GB dist*—Warner Brothers-First National.

'John Gillespie, a publisher who is ruined financially when his partner absconds with the money, appeals unsuccessfully to a wealthy aunt for assistance. On his way home, he finds a wallet full of bank notes that has been left in a taxi, and in his despair he retains the money. That same night his aunt is found dead from the effects of poison, and her safe rifled. John is accused of the crime but is acquitted of homicide on the murderer's confession.' (*Monthly Film Bulletin* 27). Powell: 'Another Warner's Teddington quota quickie and it was a very ingenious little thriller — too ingenious . . . It's funny, when a thriller's too ingenious it becomes a little picture; when it's simple it's got a chance of being big. This was beautifully worked-out little thriller with a young actor who was coming on fast and who went to Hollywood, Patric Knowles.'

Crown v. Stevens

d—Michael Powell. *p.c*—Warner Brothers-First National. *exec. p*—Irving Asher. *sc*—Brock Williams. Based on the novel *Third Time Unlucky* by Laurence Maynell. *ph*—Basil Emmott. *ed*—Bert Bates.

Beatrix Thomsom (*Doris Stevens*), Patric Knowles (*Chris Jansen*), Reginald Purdell (*Alf*), Glennis Lorimer (*Molly*), Allan Jeayes (*Inspector Carter*), Frederick Piper (*Arthur Stevens*), Googie Withers (*Ella*), Mabel Poulton (*Mamie*), Morris Harvey (*Julius Bayleck*), Billy Watts (*Joe Andrews*), Davina Craig (*Maggie*).

66 mins. *t.s*—26 March. *rel*—3 August. *GB dist*—Warner Brothers-First National. Preserved in NFA.

'Chris Jansen, visiting a pawnbroker, finds him dead, and his employer's wife, Doris Stevens, leaving the house. She enforces silence on him, but his suspicions are strengthened when he is told of the sudden illness of her husband. Later he goes to the Stevens' house; hearing a car engine running in a locked garage, he discovers Mr Stevens nearly dead. When he challenges Mrs Stevens with causing the death of the pawnbroker, she breaks down and gives herself up to the police.' (*Kine Weekly* 2.4.36).

Jack Cardiff (born 1914), previously a child actor and camera operator, works on the first three-colour Technicolor feature to be made in Britain: *Wings of the Morning*, directed by Harold Schuster, with Ray Renahan as director of photography. With this experience, he becomes a recognised Technicolor lighting adviser, working on a number of demonstration shorts and as an operator on features, before his first film as director of photography: *A Matter of Life and Death*.

The Man Behind the Mask[*]

d—Michael Powell. p.c—Joe Rock Studios. p—Joe Rock. sc—Ian Hay, Sidney Courtenay. Adapted by Jack Byrd from the novel *The Chase of the Golden Plate* by Jacques Futrelle. ph—Ernest Palmer.

Hugh Williams (*Nick Barclay*), Jane Baxter (*June Slade*), Maurice Schwartz (*The Master*), Donald Calthrop (*Dr Walpole*), Henry Oscar (*Officer*), Peter Gawthorne (*Lord Slade*), Kitty Kelly (*Miss Weeks*), Ronald Ward (*Jimmy Slade*), George Merritt (*Mallory*), Reginald Tate (*Hayden*), Ivor Bernard (*Hewitt*), Hal Gordon (*Sergeant*), Gerald Fielding (*Harah*), Barbara Everest (*Lady Slade*), Wilf Caithness (*Butler*), Moyra Fagan (*Nora*), Sid Crossley (*Postman*).

79 mins. t.s—24 March. rel—24 August. GB dist—MGM.

'Nick Barclay is assaulted on the night he is to elope from a masked ball with June Slade by a masked man who takes his place, elopes with June and steals the shield of Kahm, which June's father, Lord Slade, had recently acquired for his famous collection. Nick, now under suspicion for the theft, traces June and her kidnapper and finds the shield, but is then lured with June, now his wife, and Lord Slade to the house of a maniac international crook who had instigated the theft. The police arrive in time to save them and arrest the crook.' (*Monthly Film Bulletin* 28). Powell: 'They had a very poor script. I did my best to make it into a rather German type expressionistic thriller. It was very hard work indeed because we had no money and were working in the Rock Studios at Elstree which had been the Blattner studios. The only good that came out of it was that I met Joe Rock and I had been trying to sell my idea for *The Edge of the World* for five years.'

In May, Powell is encouraged by Joe Rock to write a script for his long-planned film about the depopulation of the Scottish islands, first suggested by a newspaper report of the evacuation of St Kilda in 1930. With backing from Joe Rock, he takes a unit to the remote island of Foula in the Shetlands and shoots under difficult conditions from June to October.

1936 had been a boom year: it was calculated that some £4 million was invested in British film production, marking the climax of a rapid expansion since 1933 (the year of Korda's *Henry VIII*). Hundreds of new production companies were being formed, studio space was increased vastly and cinema attendances were higher than ever. The Board of Trade appointed the Moyne Committee to consider the relationship between 'production, renting and exhibition', in anticipation of a new Films Act needed in 1938.

1937 The production boom had been based on optimism about the American market (unfounded) and heavy speculative borrowing (some £7 million by 1937). In January a report in *World Film News* reveals the extent of borrowing and precipitates a crisis of financial confidence. Loans are called in and small companies start to go under: George Elvin, Secretary of the ACT, reckoned that only twenty of the 640 production companies registered in the previous decade survived the crisis. Twickenham Studios goes bankrupt, Gaumont-British announce heavy losses and Korda introduces pay cuts, as the Prudential demand greater economy. Meanwhile, American companies take advantage of the situation to consolidate their position and increase investment, anticipating that a new quota act will require higher quality production.

Arthur Rank and Lady Yule split up, she and Corfield remain with British National, while Rank becomes Chairman of Pinewood Studios and takes his first steps in linking production with distribution (through GFD).

The Edge of the World

d—Michael Powell. *p.c*—Rock Studios. *p*—Joe Rock. *sc*—Michael Powell. *ph*—Ernest Palmer, Skeets Kelly, Monty Berman. *ed*—Derek Twist. *m.d*—Cyril Ray. *orchestrations*—W L Williamson. *chorus*—Women of the Glasgow Orpheus Choir. *sd*—L K Tregallas. *sd rec*—W H O Sweeny. *p.manager*—Gerard Blattner. *p. assistants*—A Seabourne, Vernon Sewell, W H Farr, George Black, W Osborne, Sydney Streeter.

John Laurie (*Peter Manson*), Belle Chrystall (*Ruth Manson*), Eric Berry (*Robbie Manson*), Kitty Kirwan (*Jean Manson*), Finlay Currie (*James Gray*), Niall MacGinnis (*Andrew Gray*), Grant Sutherland (*The Catechist*), Campbell Robson (*The Laird*), George Summers (*Skipper*), Margaret Grieg (*Baby*), Michael Powell (*Yachtsman*).

81 mins. *t.s*—6 July. *rel*—10 January 1938 (pre-release in London—September 1937). *GB dist*—British Independent Exhibitors (Distribution). *US rel*—9 September 1938. 74 mins. *US dist*—Pax Films *GB re-issue*—December 1940. 62 mins. Preserved in NFA.

Powell: '*Edge of the World* was entirely saved for me by the editor. I'd lived on the island with my crew for four months and shot a great deal of footage. I knew what I was doing and that it needed a bloody good editor. I mean, Flaherty with no story — at least I had a semblance of a story — took about six months to cut *Man of Aran*, and then it wasn't any good. He had to go away, have a refresher course, and come back and cut it again. But I didn't have six months, I had to get it cut quickly and I tried with the cutter who was on the film . . . After months, I went to Joe Rock and said, "Joe I need an editor", and he said, "Jesus Christ! What have you been doing for the last two months?" I said, "I want this boy Derek Twist", who was one of Ian Dalrymple's men from Gaumont British and who had saved *Phantom Light* . . . so he came in on the final cut of *Edge of the World* and did a great job.'

Edge of the World opens in London at the New Gallery Cinema and, among generally respectful reviews, C A Lejeune compares it with *Man of Aran* and *Turn of the Tide:* 'The same clean, primitive honesty is in all of them. But *The Edge of the World*, I believe, is in every way the more successful picture. It is, in a degree that the other two were not, a picture-maker's picture. It is full of the tricks of the trade — double exposures, ghost figures, narrative fade-outs, super-impositions of sound. But the tricks are discreetly done. They point up the emphasis of the story, never disfigure it.' (*School Master and Woman Teacher's Chronicle*, 23.9.37).

Powell considers going to America, but his agent arranges for Korda to see *Edge of the World*, which leads to Powell being offered a one-year contract. He travels to Burma to research locations for a proposed film to be written by the diplomat Sir Robert Vanstittart (*Burmese Silver*), but the project is cancelled.

1938 Emeric Pressburger is now associated with London Films and, with the arrival as a refugee of his former producer from Ufa, Günther Stapenhorst, he scripts the story of the mountaineer Edward Whymper. *The Challenge* was directed by Luis Trenker and Milton Rosmer, and photographed by Périnal and Albert Benitz. Trenker, another emigré German who had specialised in 'mountain films', also starred.

Powell publishes an account of the making of *Edge of the World*, entitled *200,000 feet on Foula* (London). The ACT quote from it in a letter to the President of the Board of Trade on the state of the industry: 'To us in the film industry it is a vivid revelation of our own unexpressed feelings, and I applaud Powell on his sincerity when he speaks of the worth of his British unit: "I have a weakness — only I think it is a strong point . . . I believe in giving young men a chance" . . . We don't shout our admiration of our fellow technicians — perhaps we are at fault in that — but we feel and know that Powell is right when he says "No one man ever made a film. He can inspire it. He can stamp his personality on it. But in the long run it is good team work that makes a good film".'

The new Films Act continues the British quota system, although with lower percentages, and seeks to improve the quality of domestic production by introducing a minimum cost level to qualify for quota recognition (£7500) and a scale of quota privileges based on production values. The Act also legislates conditions of employment for film workers and establishes the Cinematograph Films Council, with twenty-two members representing all sectors of the industry. However, two main recommendations of the Moyne

Committee are not taken up: the creation of a Films Commission to oversee the operation of the Act's provisions, and a government-sponsored scheme to secure production finance (City investment had by now almost ceased after the crisis and revelations of 1937). One immediate result of the new Act is a higher level of US investment and penetration as the major companies prepares to meet — and circumvent — the revised quota requirements.

Korda is responsible for bringing Powell and Pressburger together to develop a subject acceptable to the distinguished German actor, Conrad Veidt, who was under contract to Korda. Pressburger reworks an existing script in partnership with Powell.

1939 The Spy in Black

d—Michael Powell. p.c—Harefield. presented by—Alexander Korda. p—Irving Asher. sc—Emeric Pressburger, from Roland Pertwee's adaptation of a novel by J Storer Clouston. ph—Bernard Browne. sup ed—William Hornbeck. ed—Hugh Stewart. asst. ed—John Guthrie. p designer—Vincent Korda. a.d—Frederick Pusey. m—Miklos Rozsa. m.d—Muir Mathieson. sd—A W Watkins.

Conrad Veidt (Captain Hardt), Valerie Hobson (Schoolmistress), Sebastian Shaw (Lt Ashington), Marius Goring (Lt Schuster), June Duprez (Anne Burnett), Athole Stewart (Rev Hector Matthews), Agnes Laughlin (Mrs Matthews), Helen Haye (Mrs Sedley), Cyril Raymond (Rev John Harris), Hay Petrie (Engineer), Grant Sutherland (Bob Bratt), Robert Rendel (Admiral), Mary Morris (Chauffeuse), George Summers (Captain Ratter), Margaret Moffatt (Kate), Kenneth Warrington (Cdr Denis), Torin Thatcher (Submarine Officer), Bernard Miles, Esma Cannon, Skelton Knaggs.

82 mins. t.s—15 March. GB rel—12 August. GB/US dist—Columbia. US rel—7 October. US title—U Boat 29. Preserved in NFA.

Powell: 'It was a war film about the First World War and about getting into Scapa Flow, and it was put on at the Odeon just before the war broke out. It was about this heroic German spy ring and submarines: during the run of the picture a submarine did get into Scapa Flow and torpedoed one of our best battle ships. It just made people go more, because at least is was about what was happening. It was such a success that it was immediately retitled U Boat 29 and sent to America, where it cleaned up.'

The Prudential have been withdrawing support for London Films in face of Korda's extravagance (£1 million liabilities); they now take control of Denham Studios away from Korda. Rank forms a holding company to run both Pinewood and Denham, although Korda continues as a tenant, and retains a controlling interest in Denham laboratories.

Korda starts work on the first of a projected series of 'super productions', The Thief of Bagdad, which is to be an extravagant spectacle making full use of Technicolor and special effects. Ludwig Berger is hired as director but from the start Korda tries to bypass him and enhance the production.

Powell is appointed co-director and starts shooting scenes with Sabu and Veidt.

2 September: the day after the invasion of Poland, Korda announces that his whole staff will work on an urgent propaganda film about the Air Force and the country's preparation for war. Powell goes to Mildenhall to film the first bomber raid of the war, and then to Hornchurch to cover fighter operations.

The Lion Has Wings

d—Michael Powell, Brian Desmond Hurst, Adrian Brunel. *p.c*—London Film Productions. *p*—Alexander Korda. *assoc p*—Ian Dalrymple. *p. manager*—David Cunynghame. *sc*—Adrian Brunel, E V H Emmett, from a story by Ian Dalrymple. *ph*—Harry Stradling. *addit. ph*—Osmond Borrodaile. *cam. op*—Bernard Browne. *a.d*—Vincent Korda. *sup. ed*—William Hornbeck. *ed*—Henry Cornelius, Charles Frend. *m*—Richard Addinsell. *m.d*—Muir Mathieson. *sd*—A W Watkins. *tech. adv*—Squadron Leader H M S Wright.

Merle Oberon (*Mrs Richardson*), Ralph Richardson (*W C Richardson*), June Duprez (*June*), Robert Douglas (*Briefing Officer*), Anthony Bushell (*Pilot*), Derrick de Marney (*Bill*), Brian Worth (*Bobby*), Austin Trevor (*Schulemburg*), Ivan Brandt (*Officer*), G H Mulcaster (*Controller*), Herbert Lomas (*Holveg*), Milton Rosmer (*Head of Observer Corps*), Robert Rendel (*Chief of Air Staff*). E V H Emmett (*Narrator — English version*), Lowell Thomas (*Narrator — US version*), Archibald Batty (*Air Officer*), Ronald Adam, John Longden, Ian Fleming, Miles Malleson, Bernard Miles, Charles Garson, John Penrose, Frank Tickle.

76 mins. *t.s*—17 October. *GB rel*—3 November. *GB/US dist*—United Artists. *US rel*—19 January 1940. Preserved in NFA.

Dalrymple: 'Whether it was Alex's own idea or whether he had been unofficially urged to make it, I don't know: what I do know is that he had no financial help from the Government: that, as his normal finance was tied up in major product awaiting exhibition, to complete the film he had to pawn his last Life Insurance Policy: that those working on it received token fees, and it was released to Exhibitors on minimal terms: finally, that apart from technical guidance, the content was spontaneous — nothing in it had been imposed by the Central Authorities . . . Michael Powell dealt with Fighter Command, Brian Desmond Hurst with Bomber; the GPO Film Unit supplied material from factories overnight; Alex himself inserted one or two staged sequences with Merle Oberon and Ralph Richardson, and our excellent American film editor, William Hornbeck, and I compiled a rude opening sequence denigrating Nazism . . . after five or six weeks, we projected the show copy of a feature-length film to the inaugural chiefs of the Ministry of Information, to their stupefaction as to how the film had happened.' (Speech at conference, 'Film Propaganda and the Historian', Imperial War Museum, London 1973).

Michael Balcon, who had spent several years as head of MGM production in Britain before joining Ealing Studios in 1938, mounts a successful campaign to prevent the British quota being waived in wartime. It remains at 15% throughout the war.

1940 Contraband

d—Michael Powell. p.c—British National. p—John Corfield. assoc. p—Roland Gillett. p. manager—Anthony Nelson Keys. sc—Emeric Pressburger, Michael Powell. Based on a screenplay by Brock Williams, from a story by Pressburger. ph—F A Young. ed—John Seabourne. a.d—Alfred Junge. m—Richard Addinsell. m.d—Muir Mathieson. sd—C C Stevens.

Conrad Veidt (Captain Andersen), Valerie Hobson (Mrs Sorensen), Hay Petrie (Mate of SS Helving/Chef of 'Three Vikings'), Esmond Knight (Mr Pidgeon), Raymond Lovell (Van Dyne), Charles Victor (Hendrick), Henry Wolston (1st Danish Waiter), Julian Vedey (2nd Danish Waiter), Sydney Moncton (3rd Danish Waiter), Hamilton Keen (4th Danish Waiter), Phoebe Kershaw (Miss Lang), Leo Genn (1st Brother Grimm), Stuart Lathan (2nd Brother Grimm), Peter Bull (3rd Brother Grimm), Dennis Arundell (Lieman), Harold Warrender (Lt Cmdr Ellis RN), Joss Ambler (Lt Cmdr Ashton RNR), Molly Hamley Clifford (Baroness Hekla), Eric Berry (Mr Abo), Olga Edwards (Mrs Abo), Tony Gable (Mrs Karoly), Desmond Jeans (1st Karoly), Eric Hales (2nd Karoly), Jean Roberts (Hanson), Manning Whiley (Manager of 'Mousetrap'), Eric Maturin, John Longden (Passport Officers), Paddy Browne (Singer in 'Regency').

92 mins. t.s—20 March. GB rel—May. GB dist—Anglo. US rel—29 November. US dist—United Artists. US title—Blackout. 80 mins. Preserved in NFA.

Powell: 'Contraband was a deliberate quick pick-up by Emeric and myself. It was quite well-made — the story was pretty contrived — but it was a well-made thriller. I made it good by having all sorts of different atmospheres in it, and Emeric had some pretty good comedy ideas. The busts of Chamberlain and the dual role of the mate on the ship and the head waiter in London, they were Emeric's. We were in production and shooting within two months, and of course this was the first time in history that a blacked-out city had been put on the screen, with all the gags about 'count ten after you come up from the dark', and all the headlights masked. It made a marvellous atmosphere.'

The Film Section of the Ministry of Information, initially under Kenneth Clark, decides to sponsor feature films as propaganda. Powell and Pressburger are the first (and only) beneficiaries of this plan, which enables them to go to Canada to prepare a film intended to alert American public opinion and counter isolationism.

October 3, John Maxwell of Associated British dies and Rank acquires a controlling interest in Gaumont-British.

Work on The Thief of Bagdad had proceeded fitfully and is finally completed in Hollywood, in time for release at Christmas. Korda is to spend much of the next two years travelling between London and Hollywood.

The Thief of Bagdad

d—Ludwig Berger, Michael Powell, Tim Whelan *uncredited* Zoltan Korda, William Cameron Menzies, Alexander Korda *p.c*—London Film Productions. *p*—Alexander Korda. *assoc. p*—Zoltan Korda, William Cameron Menzies. *p. manager*—David Cunynghame. *p. asst*—André de Toth. *asst. d*—Geoffrey Boothby, Charles David. *sc*—Lajos Biro. *adapt/dial*—Miles Malleson. *ph*—Georges Perinal. *col*—Technicolor. *ext. ph*—Osmond Borrodaile. *cam op*—Robert Krasker. *sp. ph. effects*—Lawrence Butler. *Technicolor d*—Natalie Kalmus. *sup. ed*—William Hornbeck. *ed*—Charles Crichton. *a.d*—Vincent Korda. *assoc. a.d*—W Percy Day, William Cameron Menzies, Frederick Pusey, Ferdinand Bellan. *m*—Miklos Rozsa. *m.d*—Muir Mathieson. *cost*—Oliver Messel, John Armstrong, Marcel Vertes. *sd*—A W Watkins.

Conrad Veidt (*Jaffar*), Sabu (*Abu*), June Duprez (*Princess*), John Justin (*Ahmad*), Rex Ingram (*Djinni*), Miles Malleson (*Sultan*), Morton Selten (*King*), Mary Morris (*Halima*), Bruce Winston (*Merchant*), Hay Petrie (*Astrologer*), Roy Emmerton (*Jailer*), Allan Jeayes (*Storyteller*), Adelaide Hall (*Singer*).

106 mins. *t.s*—24 December. *GB/US rel*—25 December. *GB/US dist*—United Artists. *prizes*—Academy Awards for Color Cinematography, Color Art Direction, Special Effects.

Powell: 'Berger had made this very famous version of *Cinderella* and he was a tremendously stylised director, having experience in the theatre, and Korda realised he wasn't going to get the film he wanted. So he sent for me and said, 'I want you to start on some sequences down in Cornwall with Sabu and the shipwreck and the bottle: go and work them out with the crew' . . . Vincent Korda would go away and build a set. Alex would come and look at it and say, 'Vincent, you are crazy! Go away, get a lot of men, build it four times as big and paint it all crimson. It stinks.' And Vincent would ram his hat over his eyes and go off and that was how *The Thief* was built up colourwise. Meanwhile I was handed a huge ship which was supposed to be at sea amidst storms and was firmly grounded on the lot in Denham. It was the wrong type of ship to arrive in an Arabian port anyway so, having been out there researching *Burmese Silver*, the first thing I did was to have the painter paint an enormous eye on the front of the ship, like Arabs usually do. I figured people would be looking at the eye and not notice that the ship was all wrong and then I lined up a highly elaborate tracking shot which approached the ship swarming with people, went right into the eye and then away again, to give the impression that the ship was sailing towards and past us . . . There were a lot of other big sets which had to be organised into marvellous shots, and I was working on all this.'

1941 An Airmen's Letter to His Mother

A 5 minute short, based on a letter which had appeared in *The Times* from a pilot killed in action, produced and largely shot by Powell. Bernard Browne assisted with photography and John Gielgud read the letter. The film is released by MGM in early June.

49th Parallel

d—Michael Powell. *p.c*—Ortus Films/Ministry of Information. *p*—Michael Powell. *assoc. p*—Roland Gillett, George Brown. *p. sup*—Harold Boxall. *asst. d*—A Seabourne. *sc*—Emeric Pressburger. *dial*—Rodney Ackland. *ph*—Frederick Young. *cam. op*—Skeets Kelly, Henry Creer. *ed*—David Lean. *assoc. ed*—Hugh Stewart. *a.d*—David Rawnsley. *m*—Ralph Vaughan Williams. *m.d*—Muir Mathieson. *sd*—C C Stevens. *Canadian adviser*—Nugent M Cloucher.

Eric Portman (*Lieutenant Hirth*), Richard George (*Kommandant Bernsdorff*), Raymond Lovell (*Lt Kuhnecker*), Niall MacGinnis (*Vogel*), Peter Moore (*Kranz*), John Chandos (*Lohrmann*), Basil Appleby (*Jahner*), Laurence Olivier (*Johnnie, the trapper*), Finlay Currie (*Factor*), Ley On (*Nick the Eskimo*), Anton Walbrook (*Peter*), Glynis Johns (*Anna*), Charles Victor (*Andreas*), Frederick Piper (*David*), Leslie Howard (*Philip Armstrong Scott*), Tawera Moana (*George the Indian*), Eric Clavering (*Art*), Charles Rolfe (*Bob*), Raymond Massey (*Andy Brock*), Theodore Salt, O W Fonger (*US Customs Officers*).

123 mins. *t.s*—8 October. *Gb rel*—24 November. *GB dist*—GFD. *US rel*—15 April 1942. 104 mins. *US dist*—Columbia. US title—*The Invaders*. *Prizes*—Emeric Pressburger received an Oscar for the script of *49th Parallel*. Preserved in NFA.

Powell: 'The Treasury of course were madly against this and hated the film. Imagine at the time when we came back [from Canada] — France was falling, the Battle of Britain was looming — and here's some bastard who wants £50,000 or £80,000 to go and make a film in Canada. I told Duff Cooper what the scope of the film was, that we'd got promises from Laurence Olivier, Elizabeth Bergner [later replaced by Glynis Johns], Leslie Howard, Anton Walbrook, to each appear in episodes of the film, and showed him the rough story with a map of Canada. In the end, Duff Cooper stood up and said to the Treasury, 'Finance must not stand in the way of this project' . . . Financially, it was an enormous success. We had a very tiny percentage and we had to fight like hell for that . . . But of course what did annoy us was when a chap who was pretty shrewd crossed the road in Wardour Street to Arthur Rank and Oscar Deutsch and sold them on the idea and picked up some change on that; then went over to Columbia and sold it to them for America for £5000 and made much more than we ever did. Columbia handled it and called it *The Invaders* and again made a fortune out of it. I think they must have grossed £2 million.'

Rank becomes chairman of Gaumont-British. Following the deaths of Oscar Deutsch in December, he also takes over as Chairman of Odeon and assumes day-to-day control of his cinema empire. John Davis, an accountant, becomes his chief executive.

1942 One of Our Aircraft Is Missing

d—Michael Powell. *p.c*—British National. *p*—John Corfield, Michael Powell, Emeric Pressburger. *sc*—Emeric Pressburger, Michael Powell.

ph—Ronald Neame. *cam. op*—Robert Krasker, Guy Green. *ed*—David Lean. *a.d*—David Rawnsley. *sd*—C C Stevens.

Godfrey Tearle (*Sir George Corbett*), Eric Portman (*Tom Earnshaw*), Hugh Williams (*Frank Shelley*), Bernard Miles (*Geoff Hickman*), Hugh Burden (*John Glyn Haggard*), Emrys Jones (*Bob Ashley*), Pamela Brown (*Els Meertens*), Joyce Redman (*Jet Van Dieren*), Googie Withers (*Jo de Vries*), Hay Petrie (*Burgomaster*), Selma van Dias (*Burgomaster's wife*), Arnold Marle (*Pieter Sluys*), Robert Helpmann (*De Jong*), Peter Ustinov (*The Priest*), Alec Clunes (*Organist*), Hector Abbas (*Driver*), James Carson (*Louis*), Bill Akkerman (*Willem*), Joan Akkerman (*Maartje*), Peter Schenke (*Hendrik*), Valerie Moon (*Jannie*), John Salew (*Sentry*), William D'Arcy (*Officer*), David Ward (*1st Airman*), Robert Duncan (*2nd Airman*), Roland Culver (*Naval Officer*), Robert Beatty (*Hopkins*), Michael Powell (*Despatching Officer*), Stewart Rome.

102 mins. *t.s*—18 March. *GB rel*—27 June. *GB dist*—Anglo. *US rel*—16 October. 82 mins. *US dist*—United Artists.

Powell: 'All our pictures arose from thinking along the lines of either what was happening now or what was going to happen. We hadn't finished *49th Parallel* when I said to Emeric, "Does it interest you — the title *One of Our Aircraft Failed to Return?*", which was the current phrase on the radio at that time. He said, "It's an interesting idea", and then he thought up this story: "Let's show what happens to a crew when they bale out over occupied territory". By that time the phrase had changed and it was "One of our aircraft is missing".'

After a meeting with Rank at Denham, Powell and Pressburger start their own production company, The Archers, while Rank establishes Independent Producers (Production Managers [BFM] Ltd) to handle business and legal aspects of production within the Rank group by independents. The original board of Production Managers — Rank, Marcel Hellman (a Rumanian producer), Powell and Pressburger, Leslie Howard, A W Watkins — is later joined by Gabriel Pascal (producer of *Caesar and Cleopatra*), Sidney Gilliat and Frank Launder (Individual Pictures); David Lean, Anthony Havelock-Allan and Ronald Neame (Cineguild); Ian Dalrymple (Wessex). Thus Rank aims to occupy his studios and provide British films for his now vast cinema chains.

Powell and Pressburger plan their next film, originally titled *The Life and Death of 'Sugar' Candy,* suggested by a (cut) scene from *One of Our Aircraft.* The elderly rear gunner (Godfrey Tearle) says to the young pilot (Hugh Burden): 'You wouldn't know anything about it, but you've got exactly the same sort of mentality and character that I had when I was young and I tell you that in forty years you'll be just like me, a crusty old bugger'. Now titled *The Life and Death of Colonel Blimp,* the project runs into official opposition (see Part 4) army facilities are denied and Laurence Olivier, cast as Blimp, is not released from service. However, with Rank's support, production goes ahead.

1943 His Majesty's Stationery Office publish a 32pp illustrated booklet based on *One of Our Aircraft*. The story is told in the first person by Sir George Corbett.

The Silver Fleet

d—Vernon C Sewell, Gordon Wellesley. *p.c*—The Archers. *p*—Michael Powell, Emeric Pressburger. *assoc. p*—Ralph Richardson. *sc*—Vernon C Sewell, Gordon Wellesley. *ph*—Erwin Hillier. *cam. op*—Cecil Cooney. *ed*—Michael C Chorlton. *p. designer*—Alfred Junge. *m*—Allan Gray. *sd*—John Dennis, Desmond Dew.

Ralph Richardson (*Jaap van Leyden*), Googie Withers (*Helene van Leyden*), Esmond Knight (*von Schiffer*), Beresford Egan (*Krampf*), Frederick Burtwell (*Càptain Muller*), Kathleen Byron (*Schoolmistress*), Willem Akkerman (*Willem van Leyden*), Dorothy Gordon (*Janni Peters*), Charles Victor (*Bastiaan Peters*), John Longden (*Jost Meertens*), Joss Ambler (*Cornelius Smit*), Margaret Emden (*Bertha*), George Schelderup (*Dirk*), Neville Mapp (*Joop*), Ivor Barnard (*Admiral*), John Carol (*Johann*), Phillip Leaver (*Chief of Police*), Laurence o'Madden (*Captain Schneider*), Anthony Eustrel (*Lt Wernicke*), Charles Minor (*Bohme*), Valentine Dyall (*Markgraf*), Lt Schouwenaar (*U-Boat Captain*), Lt van Dapperen (*U-Boat Lieutenant*), John Arnold (*U-Boat Navigator*), and personnel of the Royal Netherlands Navy.

88 mins. *t.s*—24 February. *GB rel*—15 March. *GB dist*—GFD. *US rel*—1 July 1945. 81 mins. *US dist*—Producers Releasing Corporation. Preserved in NFA.

Sewell had been directing and scripting features since 1934, and captained the supply ship for *Edge of the World*. Powell recalls that he was closely involved in the planning of *The Silver Fleet* which, with its Dutch resistance subject, is developed from *One of Our Aircraft*.

The Life and Death of Colonel Blimp

d/p/sc—Michael Powell, Emeric Pressburger. *p.c*—The Archers/Independent Producers. *ph*—Georges Périnal. *col*—Technicolor. *cam. op*—Jack Cardiff, Geoffrey Unsworth. *ed*—John Seabourne. *p. designer*—Alfred Junge. *m*—Allan Gray. *sd*—C C Stevens. *military adviser*—Lt General Sir Douglas Brownrigg.

Anton Walbrook (*Theo Kretschmar-Schuldorff*), Roger Livesey (*Clive Candy*), Deborah Kerr (*Edith/Barbara/Angela*), Roland Culver (*Colonel Betteridge*), James McKechnie (*Spud Wilson*), Albert Lieven (*von Ritter*), Arthur Wontner (*Counsellor*), David Hutcheson (*Hoppy*), Ursula Jeans (*Frau Kalteneck*), John Laurie (*Murdoch*), Harry Welchman (*Major Davis*), Reginald Tate (*Van Zijl*), A E Matthews (*President*), Carl Jaffe (*von Reumann*), Valentine Dyall (*von Schonbron*), Muriel Aked (*Aunt Margaret*), Felix Aylmer (*Bishop*), Frith Banbury (*Babyface Fitzroy*), Neville Mapp (*Graves*), Vincent Holman (*Club Porter, 1942*), Spencer Trevor (*Period Blimp*), Dennis Arundell (*Café Orchestra Leader*), James Knight (*Club Porter, 1902*), David Ward (*Kaunitz*), Jan van Loewen (*Indignant Citizen*),

Eric Maturin (*Colonel Goodhead*), Robert Harris (*Embassy Secretary*), Count Zichy (*Colonel Berg*), Jane Millican (*Nurse Erna*), Phyllis Morris (*Pebble*), Diana Marshall (*Sybil*), Captain W Barrett (*The Texan*), Corporal Thomas Palmer (*Sergeant*), Yvonne Andre (*Nun*), Marjorie Greasley (*Matron*), Helen Debray (*Mrs Wynne*), Norman Pierce (*Mr Wynne*), Edward Cooper (*BBC Official*), Joan Swinstead (*Secretary*).

163 mins (later cut to ca 140 and 120 mins). *t.s*—8 June. *GB rel*—26 July (Charity Premiere 10 June). *GB dist*—GFD. *US rel*—4 May 1945. 148 mins (?) *US dist*—United Artists. Preserved in NFA.

Powell: 'It was almost all shot in London and when it wasn't the detail was all authentic. That was the first film that I worked directly on with Alfred Junge. He had a lot to do with the first film I made for Mickey Balcon, *The Night of the Party*; he was head art director at Balcon's Lime Grove studio. He was interned like other enemy aliens, then screened and let out, and as soon as I knew we were going to do *Colonel Blimp* I leapt for Junge and Périnal . . . [On use of Technicolor:] It was in Mrs Kalmus' contract that every costume, every material, every important prop had to be OK'd by her representative and they got away with this up until I did *Colonel Blimp*. It's Emeric's favourite picture and his best.'

The Ministry of Information obstructs export of *Colonel Blimp* until late in the year (see Part 4).

The Volunteer

d/p//sc—Michael Powell, Emeric Pressburger. *p.c*—The Archers. *ph*—Freddie Ford. *ed*—John Seabourne. *m*—Allan Gray.

Ralph Richardson (*Himself*), Pat McGrath (*Fred Davey*), Laurence Olivier, Michael Powell.

46 mins. *t.s*—5 November. *rel*—10 January 1944. *dist*—Anglo.

Ralph Richardson is taking part in a production of *Othello:* he is seen in scenes from the play and backstage with his dresser. Other scenes show costumed actors in a film studio canteen. Richardson and his dresser both join the Fleet Air Arm. Powell: 'It was a fairly complicated story within a story and the episodes [Emeric] wanted were difficult to obtain — we were a bit early for that sort of thing.'

1944 Powell directs a production of the play *Fifth Column* by Ernest Hemmingway, with Roger Livesey, at the Theatre Royal Glasgow and on tour.

A Canterbury Tale

d/p/sc—Michael Powell, Emeric Pressburger. *p.c*—The Archers. *ph*—Erwin Hillier. *ed*—John Seabourne. *p. designer*—Alfred Junge. *m*—Allan Gray. *cond*—Walter Goehr.

Eric Portman (*Thomas Culpepper, JP*), Sheila Sim (*Allison Smith*), Sgt John Sweet (*Bob Johnson*), Dennis Price (*Peter Gibbs*), Esmond Knight (*Narrator/Seven-Sisters Soldier/Village Idiot*), Charles Hawtrey (*Thomas Duckett*), Hay Petrie (*Woodcock*), George Merrit (*Neg Horton*), Edward

Rigby (*Jim Horton*), Freda Jackson (*Prudence Honeywood*), Betty Jardine (*Fee Baker*), Eliot Makeham (*Organist*), Harvey Golden (*Sgt Roczinsky*), Leonard Smith (*Leslie*), James Tamsitt (*Terry*), David Todd (*David*).

124 mins. *t.s*—9 May, *GB rel*—21 August. *GB dist*—Eagle-Lion. *US rel*—21 January 1949. 95 mins. Preserved in NFA.

Powell: 'At the time no-body thought that *A Canterbury Tale* worked, but I must say that it contained some of my favourite sequences . . . you take the last three reels of the film when all the pilgrims converge on Canterbury, I thought that had a most wonderful movement. But it was one of Emeric's most complicated ideas and I really let him down by not insisting that it was simplified. The other sequence I liked was that in the blacksmith's shop, which was beautifully written, but the story itself had an impossible premise. Things like the sequence on the skyscraper were put in afterwards as a desperate attempt to sell it.' [Powell refers here to the shortened version, which places the story in flashback as the American sergeant later tells his wife about it. The original version was restored by the National Film Archive in 1977.]

The Palache Report, 'Tendencies to Monopoly in the Cinematograph Film Industry', results from pressure by Michael Balcon and others on the Films Council to investigate the growth of the Rank empire and the integration of production, distribution and exhibition interests. The report sees monopoly as 'a threat to the future prospects of an independent and unfettered British film industry. By "independent" we have in mind both freedom from foreign domination and freedom from dominating British control.' It concludes that the survival of British production is 'dependent on two persons, the head of Gaumont-British-Odeon and the head of Associated British Pictures. Moreover, these two persons are or may ultimately be guided by American interests.' Despite the committee's warning against monopoly and 'undesirable practices in restraint of trade', no immediate action is taken on the report. Rank claims that he has never heard the words 'vertically integrated combine' until Balcon used them, and does not know what they mean. Balcon's term on the Films Council is not renewed by the President of the Board of Trade, Hugh Dalton.

1945 I Know Where I'm Going

d/p/sc—Michael Powell, Emeric Pressburger. *p.c*—The Archers. *assoc. p*—George R Busby. *ph*—Erwin Hillier. *ed*—John Seabourne. *a.d*—Alfred Junge. *m*—Allan Gray. *sd*—C C Stevens.

Wendy Hillier (*Joan Webster*), Roger Livesey (*Torquil MacNeil*), George Carney (*Mr Webster*), Pamela Brown (*Catriona*), Walter Hudd (*Hunter*), Capt Duncan MacKechnie (*Captain 'Lochinvar'*), Ian Sadler (*Ian*), Finlay Currie (*Ruairidh Mor*), Murdo Morrison (*Kenny*), Margot Fitzsimmons (*Bridie*), Capt C W R Knight (*Colonel Barnstaple*), Donald Strachan (*Sheperd*), John Rae (*Old Shepherd*), Duncan MacIntyre (*His Son*), Jean Cadell (*Postmistress*), Norman Shelley (*Sir Robert Bellinger*), Ivy Milton (*Peigi*), Anthony Eustrel (*Hooper*), Petula Clark (*Cheril*), Alec Faversham (*Martin*), Catherine Lacey (*Mrs Robinson*), Valentine Dyall (*Mr Robinson*),

Nancy Price (*Mrs Crozier*), Herbert Lomas (*Mr Campbell*), Kitty Kirwan (*Mrs Campbell*), John Laurie (*John Campbell*), Graham Moffat (*RAF Sergeant*), Boyd Stevens, Maxwell Kennedy, Jean Houston (*Singers in the Ceildhe*), Arthur Chesney (*Harmonica Player*).

92 mins. *t.s*—30 October. *GB rel*—17 December. *GB dist*—GFD. *US rel*—9 August 1947. *US dist*—Universal. Preserved in NFA.

Powell: '*I Know Where I'm Going* was eventually a successful film, but I don't think it ever made money. In those days if a film didn't click right away — as Rank didn't have world-wide distribution and had to depend on the charity of the Americans — it was very unlikely to make money. Arthur Rank wrote me a letter about it saying that he liked this and this, and that it must still be possible to make films like it and make money. When the Americans saw it they immediately put it on the shelf. About a year later they put it on in Boston because it had an Irish tune in it: naturally it wasn't a success. But when they put it on Broadway it was a great success . . . *Canterbury Tale* was made as a crusade against materialism and Emeric said, "Well let's have another go at it so we can see what's going to happen when the war is over".' Pressburger: 'Another film I like very much is *I Know Where I'm Going*. It burst out — you couldn't hold it back. I wrote the full script of that in four days and I felt strongly about the idea.

1946 Alexander Korda, after two years as head of MGM-London Films, resigns from MGM, resurrects London Film Productions in January, acquires a controlling interest in British Lion (distributors) and in April buys Shepperton Studios as his new production headquarters.

Michael Powell publishes a short essay on the question of British films and 'international appeal' in the first issue of *Penguin Film News*.

A Matter of Life and Death

d/p/sc—Michael Powell, Emeric Pressburger. *p.c*—The Archers. *assoc. p*—George R Busby. *asst. d*—Parry Jones, Jr. *ph*—Jack Cardiff. *col*—Technicolor. *cam. op*—Geoffrey Unsworth. *p. designer*—Alfred Junge. *asst. a.d*—Arthur Lawson. *ed*—Reginald Mills. *m*—Allan Gray. *cond*—W L Williamson. *cost*—Hein Heckroth. *sd*—C C Stevens.

David Niven (*Peter Carter*), Kim Hunter (*June*), Robert Coote (*Bob*), Kathleen Byron (*Angel*), Richard Attenborough (*English Pilot*), Bonar Colleano (*American Pilot*), Joan Maude (*Chief Recorder*), Marius Goring (*Conductor 71*), Roger Livesey (*Dr Reeves*), Edwin Max (*Dr McEwen*), Abraham Sofaer (*The Judge*), Raymond Massey (*Abraham Farlan*), Robert Atkins (*Vicar*), Betty Potter (*Mrs Tucker*), Bob Roberts (*Dr Gaertler*).

104 mins. *t.s*—12 November. *GB rel*—30 December. *GB dist*—GFD. *US rel*—March 1947. *US dist*—Universal. US title—*Stairway to Heaven*. Shown at the first Royal Film Performance. Preserved in NFA.

Powell: 'For me, *A Matter of Life and Death* is the most perfect film: the technical perfection and the fact that it is a most wonderful conjuring trick to get handed. It is all the more fascinating to me because all this fantasy actually takes place in a medical case, inside somebody's damaged head, so there was a good sound medical reason for every image that appeared on the screen . . . The film was actually started by the Ministry of Information sending for us saying, "Well, the war's nearly over boys, but it's just starting from our point of view. We think you should make a film about Anglo-American relations because they are deteriorating." Of course, they didn't know we would come up with *A Matter of Life and Death*.'

A 'book of the film', adapted by Eric Warman, published by World Wide Publications, London. Numerous illustrations, including production photographs set designs, portraits and stills sequences.

1947 Black Narcissus

d/p/sc—Michael Powell, Emeric Pressburger. Based on a novel by Rumer Godden. *p.c*—The Archers. *assoc. p*—George R Busby. *asst. d*—Sydney Streeter. *ph*—Jack Cardiff. *col*—Technicolor. *cam. op*—Ted Scaife. *ed*—Reginald Mills. *p. designer*—Alfred Junge. *cost*—Hein Heckroth. *m*—Brian Easdale. *sd*—Stanley Lambourne.

Deborah Kerr (*Sister Clodagh*), Sabu (*The Young General*), David Farrar (*Mr Dean*), Flora Robson (*Sister Philippa*), Esmond Knight (*The Old General*), Kathleen Byron (*Sister Ruth*), Jenny Laird (*Sister Honey*), Judith Furse (*Sister Briony*), May Hallatt (*Angu Ayah*), Shaun Noble (*Con*), Eddie Whaley Jr (*Joseph Anthony*), Nancy Roberts (*Mother Dorothea*), Jean Simmons (*Kanchi*).

100 mins. *t.s*—22 April. *GB rel*—26 May. *GB dist*—GFD. *US rel*—December. *US dist*—Universal. *prizes*—Oscar for colour cinematography.

Powell: '*Black Narcissus* I would describe as a well-made film. There again the atmosphere carefully and meticulously built up from the first decision never to go to India, which was the most important decision. These films are nearly always pastiche or hotch-potch — you know, real Southern India in the studio — so I said: "This won't do, such a delicate story, we've got to create a whole atmosphere here." Faces fell all round — they wanted to go to India but afterwards they enjoyed themselves throroughly — we had a great team by then . . . The composer was in charge of all the sound effects. This was Brian Easdale's first picture with us: he'd been in India and loved working on propaganda pictures there. He was recommended to me by Carol Reed.'

The Robsons attack Powell and Pressburger again in their book *The World is My Cinema* (Sidneyan Society, London), for purveying anti-British and anti-American propaganda. Their far-right, fundamentalist reading of *Matter of Life and Death* warns against 'naked German-Nazi-Fascist philosophy which is about to be rammed down your throat.'

Since wartime restrictions on remittance of sterling abroad were lifted in 1944, annual returns to American producers and distributors had risen to £17 million. In August, after intense speculation in face of a worsening balance of payments, the Chancellor of the Exchequer, Hugh Dalton, imposes a 75% *ad valorem* customs duty on all films imported. The Motion

Picture Association of America, representing the major studios, immediately
responds by placing an embargo on exports to Britain. For eight months the
deadlock continues and, amid exhibitors' protests and the collapse of many
small producers through distributors' withdrawal of guarantees, Rank and
Korda both announce massive production programmes to fill the gap.
Despite losses in the previous year, Rank proposes to spend £9¼ million on
forty-seven productions, while Korda speaks of thirteen at £4½ million. By
the end of the year some twenty productions are under way in British
studios; existing stocks and re-issues of American films continue to draw
large attendances; Harold Wilson, President of the Board of Trade, creates
the National Film Production Council to consider how British production
can achieve 'maximum output on a sound economic basis'; and the British
Film Academy is founded, with Roger Manvell as director and David Lean
as first chairman.

Gavin Lambert, writing on 'British Films' in the second issue of *Sequence*
(Winter 1947), deplores the element of *kitsch* in Powell and Pressburger's
films, 'yet one still feels that Powell, although he has never made an entirely
satisfactory film, remains potentially one of the most interesting British
directors.'

Powell and Pressburger discuss a project with Korda, 'The Promotion of the
Admiral'. Through The Archers they produce a film starring Sabu in an
adult part, directed by the editor Powell had brought in on *Edge of the
World*, and written by a German emigré friend of Pressburger's.

The End of the River

d—Derek Twist. *p.c*—The Archers. *p*—Michael Powell, Emeric Press-
burger. *asst. p*—George R Busby. *asst. d*—Geoffrey Lambert. *sc*—
Wolfgang Wilhelm. *ph*—Christopher Challis. *ed*—Brereton Porter. *a.d*—
Fred Pusey. *asst. a.d*—E E C Scott. *m*—Lambert Williamson. *m.d*—Muir
Mathieson. *sd*—Charles Knott.

Sabu (*Manoel*), Bibi Férreira (*Teresa*), Esmond Knight (*Dantos*), Antoinette
Cellier (*Conceicao*), Robert Douglas (*Jones*), Torin Thatcher (*Lisboa*),
Orlando Martins (*Harrigan*), Raymond Lovell (*Porpino*), James Hayter
(*Chico*), Nicolette Bernard (*Dona Serafina*), Minto Cato (*Dona Paula*),
Maurice Denham (*Defending Counsel*), Eva Hudson (*Maria Gonsalves*),
Alan Wheatley (*Irygoyen*), Charles Hawtrey (*Raphael*), Zena Marshall
(*Sante*), Dennis Arundell (*Continho*), Milton Rosmer (*The Judge*), Peter
Illing (*Ship's Agent*), Nino Rossini (*Feliciano*), Basil Appleby (*Ship's
Officer*), Milo Sperber (*Ze*), Andreas Malandrinos (*Officer of the Indian
Protection Society*), Arthur Goullet (*The Pedlar*), Russell Napier (*The
Padre*).

83 mins. *t.s*—23 October. *GB rel*—1 December. *GB dist*—Rank. *US rel*—7
July 1948 (80 mins).

1948 The new Chancellor, Stafford Cripps, repeals the 75% tax on imported films
and negotiates an Anglo-American film agreement in March which allows

American companies to remit annually up to £4 million ($17 million) of revenue earned in Britain, along with an additional amount proportional to British earnings in America, the balance to be available for re-investment — hopefully in making films in Britain. Almost immediately, the British quota is increased from 20% to 45%, but already the backlog of American films delayed by the export ban has reached Britain and Rank and Korda find that their emergency productions are faced with unequal competition. Entertainment Tax reaches new levels and claims £39 million of the £109 million taken at the box office in 1948. Rank announces to shareholders in October a £16 million overdraft and heavy production losses.

The 'independent frame' experiment at Rank is discontinued after nearly two years. Developed by the art director David Rawnsley, who had become head of Rank Research Department, this involved a radical reconsideration of traditional studio construction techniques and the increased use of mobile set components and optical effects to speed production. Powell is closely involved in this experiment, having responsibility for research 'on the camera side', and uses 'independent frame' techniques in his subsequent ballet films.

The Red Shoes

d/p/sc—Michael Powell, Emeric Pressburger. *p.c*—The Archers. *asst. p*—George Busby. *sc*—from an original screenplay by Emeric Pressburger. *ph*—Jack Cardiff. *col*—Technicolor. *cam. op*—Christopher Challis. *sp. ph. effects*—F George Dunn, D Hague (Technicolor composite photography). *ed*— Reginald Mills. *p. designer*—Hein Heckroth. *a.d*—Arthur Lawson. *m*—Brian Easdale. *m.d*—Brian Easdale, Sir Thomas Beecham. *singer*— Margherita Grandi. *dancer*—Alan Carter (also assistant *maitre-de-ballet*). *sd*—Charles Poulton. *choreo*—Robert Helpmann.

Marius Goring (*Julian Craster*), Anton Walbrook (*Boris Lermontov*), Moira Shearer (*Victoria Page*), Jean Short (*Terry*), Gordon Littman (*Ike*), Julia Lang (*Balletomane*), Bill Shine (*Her Companion*), Leonid Massine (*Ljubov*), Austin Trevor (*Professor Palmer*), Esmond Knight (*Livy*), Eric Berry (*Dimitri*), Irene Browne (*Lady Neston*), Ludmilla Tcherina (*Boronskaja*), Jerry Verno (*Stage-door Keeper*), Robert Helpmann (*Ivan Boleslawsky*), Albert Basserman (*Ratov*), Derek Elphinstone (*Lord Oldham*), Madame Rambert (*Herself*), Joy Rawlins (*Galdys, Victoria's Friend*), Marcel Poncin (*M Boudin*), Michel Bazalgette (*M Rideaut*), Yvonne Andre (*Victoria's Dresser*), Hay Petrie (*Boisson*), George Woodbridge (*Doorman*).

133 mins. *t.s*—20 July. *GB rel*—6 September. *GB dist*—GFD. *US rel*—1 October 1951. *US dist*—Universal. Preserved in NFA.

Pressburger had originally written a script at Korda's request before the war, to star Merle Oberon (whom Korda married). This Powell and Pressburger now bought back from Korda, since he was no longer interested in the project, and persuaded Rank to finance it. The film went nearly £200,000 over budget. Powell: 'When the Rank Organisation saw it they thought they were sunk. I didn't show it to Rank and John Davis, but Emeric did . . . When the film finished, they got up and left the theatre without a word because they thought they had lost their shirts. They couldn't understand one word of it. Universal were their partners and as soon as they could get a print they showed it to some executives who were quite excited about us because of *Stairway to Heaven (Matter of Life and Death)* and *Black Narcissus*. An executive stood up there and said, "This film will not make a penny." The next thing was $5 million. It's probably grossed $20 to $30 million.

The National Film Finance Company (Corporation from 1949) is launched in October, with powers to grant loans to independent producers under stringent conditions. Its first loan, urged by Sir William Eady, is £2 million to Korda's British Lion, soon followed by a further £1 million. The loan is heavily criticised, but, allowing Korda to recover from his heavy production losses of 1948, it provides a base for his future programme — much of it the work of film makers who are leaving the increasingly unsympathetic Rank organisation. Powell: 'It was perfectly natural that Alex should want to seduce us away from Rank, which was our home, but we didn't feel any special loyalty to Rank. We liked Arthur Rank very much indeed, but he didn't start us off together — Korda did.'

Lavishly illustrated book of the film, *The Red Shoes Ballet: A Critical Study* by Monk Gibbon (London, Saturn Press).

1949   The Small Back Room

d/p—Michael Powell, Emeric Pressburger. *p.c*—London Film Productions, The Archers. *asst. d*—Sydney Streeter. *sc*—Michael Powell, Emeric Pressburger, Nigel Balchin, from the novel by Nigel Balchin. *ph*—Christopher Challis. *cam. op*—Freddie Francis. *ed*—Reginald Mills, Clifford Turner. *p. designer*—Hein Heckroth. *a.d*—John Hoesli. *m*—Brian Easdale. *night-club m*—Ted Heath's Kenny Baker Swing Group. *sd*—Alan Allen.

David Farrar (*Sammy Rice*), Kathleen Byron (*Susan*), Jack Hawkins (*R B Waring*), Leslie Banks (*Colonel Holland*), Michael Gough (*Stuart*), Cyril Cusack (*Corporal Taylor*), Milton Rosmer (*Professor Mair*), Walter Fitzgerald (*Brine*), Emrys Jones (*Joe*), Michael Goodliffe (*Till*), Renee Asherson (*ATS Corporal*), Anthony Bushell (*Colonel Strang*), Henry Caine (*Sgt-Major Rose*), Elwyn Brook-Jones (*Gladwin*), James Dale (*Brigadier*), Sam Kydd (*Crowhurst*), June Elvin (*Gillian*), David Hutcheson (*Norval*), Sidney James (*Knucksie*), Roderick Lovell (*Pearson*), James Carney (*Sgt Groves*), Roddy Hughes (*Welsh Doctor*), Geoffrey Keen (*Pinker*), Bryan Forbes (*Dying Gunner*), 'A Guest' [Robert Morley] (*The Minister*).

108 mins. *t.s*—27 January. *GB rel*—21 February. *GB dist*—British Lion. *US rel*—23 February 1952. *US dist*—Snader Productions.

Powell: 'We had a contract with Korda, a very good one, but the first film which everybody liked was a failure — *The Small Back Room* was a financial failure.'

1950 As recession continues in the British film industry, the Government draws on features of the Italian and French subsidy schemes to establish the British Production Fund, or Eady Plan (after Sir William Eady, who devised it). This operates through a levy on every cinema admission, the resulting fund to be divided annually among British productions in proportion to their box office performance. From the start, 'Eady money' tempts American producers to use their frozen assets in Britain to make 'British' productions (Disney's first live-action feature, *Treasure Island,* is an early product of this situation).

Powell writes in *Picturegoer* to defend his two forthcoming films against hostile criticism from press reviewers: 'But what do they know of England who only the West End know? ... Beauty, truth and the heart of England, I believe in these three things. They are in these two books [*The Scarlet Pimpernel* and *Gone to Earth*]. And they are in the two films which we have made.'

Gone to Earth

d—Michael Powell, Emeric Pressburger. *p.c*—London Film Productions, Vanguard Productions. *pres*—Alexander Korda and David O Selznick. *p*—David O Selznick. *assoc p*—George R Busby. *asst. d*—Sydney Streeter. *sc*—Michael Powell, Emeric Pressburger, from the novel by Mary Webb. *ph*—Christopher Challis. *col*—Technicolor. *p designer*—Hein Heckroth. *a.d*—Arthur Lawson. *ed*—Reginald Mills. *m*—Brian Easdale. *sd*—Charles Poulton.

Jennifer Jones (*Hazel Woodus*), David Farrar (*Jack Reddin*), Cyril Cusack (*Edward Marston*), Sybil Thorndyke (*Mrs Marston*), Edward Chapman (*Mr James*), Esmond Knight (*Abel Woodus*), Hugh Griffith (*Andrew Vessons*), George Cole (*Albert*), Beatrice Varley (*Aunt Prowde*), Frances Clare (*Amelia Comber*), Raymond Rollett (*Landlord*), Gerald Lawson (*Roadmender*), Bartlett Mullins, Arthur Reynolds (*Chapel Elders*), Ann Tetheradge (*Miss James*), Peter Dunlop (*Cornet Player*), Louis Phillip (*Policeman*), Valentine Dunn (*Martha*), Richmond Nairne (*Mathias Brooker*) [US version only: Joseph Cotten (*Narrator*).]

110 mins. *t.s*—19 September. *GB rel*—6 November. *GB dist*—British Lion. *US rel*—July 1952 [82 mins. *addit. d*—Rouben Mamoulian.]US title—*The Wild Heart. US dist*—RKO Radio. Preserved in NFA.

Powell: '*Gone to Earth* was a production planned between Alex Korda and David Selznick, who was madly in love with Jennifer Jones. He had seen *The Red Shoes,* sent us a telegram about it; and he'd seen *Black Narcissus* and loved it even more. He was mad to make a film with us and I proposed a subject that they didn't understand; then Alex proposed the subject he owned, *Gone to Earth,* and everybody liked it. It was a disaster, I think, except for Jennifer's performance, which I thought was absolutely wonderful ... But we never licked the script — it's doubtful if Mary Webb can be licked.' Selznick was dissatisfied with the film as completed by Powell and Pressburger, and hired Mamoulian to do extensive re-shooting in America. The result, known as *The Wild Heart,* is both substantially shorter and different from *Gone to Earth*. Copies of the latter are now very rare and it is the Selznick version that is commonly shown on television and elsewhere.

The Elusive Pimpernel

d—Michael Powell, Emeric Pressburger. *p.c*—The Archers for London Film Productions. *p*—Samuel Goldwyn, Alexander Korda. *assoc. p*—George R Busby. *asst. d*—Sydney Streeter. *sc*—Michael Powell, Emeric Pressburger, from the novel by Baroness Orczy. *ph*—Christopher Challis. *col*—Technicolor. *cam. op*—Freddie Francis. *sp effects*—W Percy Day. *p designer*—Hein Heckroth. *a.d*—Arthur Lawson, Joseph Bato. *ed*—Reginald Mills. *m*—Brian Easdale. *sd*—Charles Poulton, Red Law.

David Niven (*Sir Percy Blakeney*), Margaret Leighton (*Marguerite Blakeney*), Jack Hawkins (*Prince of Wales*), Cyril Cusack (*Chauvelin*), Robert Coote (*Sir Andrew Ffoulkes*), Edmond Audran (*Armand St Juste*), Danielle Godet (*Suzanne de Tournai*), Charles Victor (*Colonel Winterbottom*), David Hutcheson (*Lord Anthony Dewhurst*), Arlette Marchal (*Contesse de Tournai*), Gerard Nery (*Phillipe de Tournai*), Eugene Deckers (*Captain Merieres*), John Longden (*Abbot*), Arthur Wontner (*Lord Grenville*), David Oxley (*Captain Duroc*), Raymond Rollett (*Bibot*), Philip Stainton (*Jellyband*), Robert Griffiths (*Trubshaw*), George de Warfaz (*Baron*), Jane Gill Davies (*Lady Grenville*), Richard George (*Sir John Coke*), Cherry Cottrell (*Lady Bristow*), John Fitzgerald (*Sir Michael Travers*), Patrick Macnee (*Hon John Bristow*), Terence Alexander (*Duke of Dorset*), Tommy Dugan (*Earl of Sligo*), John Fitchen (*Nigel Seymour*), John Hewitt (*Major Pretty*), Hugh Kelly (*Mr Fitzdrummond*), Richmond Nairne (*Beau Pepys*).

109 mins. *t.s*—9 November. *GB rel*—1 January 1951. *GB dist*—British Lion. *US rel*—floating 1955. *US dist*—Caroll Pictures. US title—*The Fighting Pimpernel*.

Powell: '*The Elusive Pimpernel* was another disaster. I never wanted to do it. It took a year to talk me into it and I wanted to make a musical of it, but Alex didn't like the idea. It never went right because there were relics of the musical idea still in it. I'd given it a completely different story line but Alex and Sam Goldwyn wanted a lot of the original story line put back again. It was a really terrible mess.'

Anton Walbrook appears in Ophuls' *La Ronde,* one of the first films to be given the British Board of Film Censors' new 'X' certificate in the following year.

1951 The Tales of Hoffmann

d/p/sc—Michael Powell, Emeric Pressburger. *p.c*—The Archers for London Film Productions. *assoc p*—George R Busby. *asst. d*—Sydney Streeter. *sc*—from Dennis Arundell's adaptation of the opera by Offenbach; libretto by Jules Barbier. *ph*—Christopher Challis. *col*—Technicolor. *p.designer/cost*—Hein Heckroth. *a.d*—Arthur Lawson. *ed*—Reginald Mills. *m*—Jacques Offenbach. *m.d*—Sir Thomas Beecham. *choreo*—Frederick Ashton.

Prologue and Epilogue: Moira Shearer (*Stella*), Robert Rounseville (*Hoffmann*), **Robert** Helpmann (*Lindorff*), Pamela Brown (*Nicklaus*), Frederick Ashton (*Kleinzack*), Meinhart Maur (*Luther*), Edmond Audran (*Cancer*).

The Tale of Olympia: Moira Shearer (*Olympia*), Robert Helpmann (*Coppelius*), Leonid Massine (*Spalanzani*).

The Tale of Giulietta: Ludmilla Tcherina (*Giulietta*), Robert Helpmann (*Dr Dapertutto*), Leonid Massine (*Schlemiel*).

The Tale of Antonia: Ann Ayars (*Antonia*), Robert Helpmann (*Dr Miracle*), Leonid Massine (*Franz*).

Singers: Owen Brannigan, Monica Sinclair, René Soames, Bruce Darvaget, Dorothy Bond, Margherita Grandi, Grahame Clifford.

127 mins (reduced to 115 mins before release). *t.s*—17 May. *GB rel*—26 November. *GB dist*—British Lion. *US rel*—13 June 1952. *US dist*—United Artists. *Prizes*—Special Jury Prize, Prize of the Commission Supérieure Technique, Cannes 1951. Preserved in NFA.

Powell: 'We were just about thinking of settling the contract [with Korda] when Tommy Beecham came up with the suggestion of *The Tales of Hoffmann,* because he wanted to make a film with us after having conducted the ballet of *The Red Shoes.* He trusted us to make a musical film. Korda loved the idea. That was a very happy picture because in many ways we got together the same team as *The Red Shoes.* The thing for me, technically, was that I agreed to make it if it was a composed film . . . When we showed it at Cannes, Korda told us that if we removed the last sequence we could take the Grand Prix but I wouldn't do that. [This sequence is now removed from the GB distribution version.] The Venetian sequence was wonderful and some of the most effective scenes were shot in half an hour. It wasn't a very expensive picture. We shot nine weeks. We shot the puppet sequences afterwards; I thought choruses and dancers would be boring.'

Powell produces a play by James Forsyth, *Héloïse,* with Siobhan McKenna and Walter Macken. Golders Green from 29 October; Duke of York's from 14 November.

Another book of the film by Monk Gibbon, *The Tales of Hoffmann: A Study of the Film* (London, Saturn Press).

'Telekinema' set up on the South Bank in London, as part of the Festival of Britain. First used to demonstrate 3-D, large screen and stereo systems, this later becomes the National Film Theatre.

Part of the Eady levy is used to establish the Children's Film Foundation, to make short features for children's matinees: these are distributed through the Rank group.

1952   'In January 1952, the English film producer Michael Powell came to see me in Hollywood with a project that I found very attractive. Powell proposed to make a short film, a kind of masque, of a scene from the *Odyssey*; it would

require two or three arias as well as pieces of pure instrumental music and recitations of pure poetry. Powell said that [Dylan] Thomas had agreed to write the verse; he asked me to compose the music. Alas, there was no money . . .'
(Robert Craft, *Conversations with Igor Stravinsky*, London 1958).

Powell: 'I thought after the success of *The Red Shoes* and *Tales of Hoffmann*, which interested painters and poets all over the world, that I could get together a group of people — painters like Picasso and Sutherland, poets like Dylan Thomas — and offer twenty hours of entertainment in colour. But some of the stories would be two hours long and some may be only minutes . . . One of the projects was this short episode from the *Odyssey* when Ulysses is washed ashore and Nausicaa and her maidens come down to the sea-shore to wash linen. They dance on the linen in order to beat it. We wanted Stravinsky to do the music and Dylan the words.'

Powell plans a film of *The Tempest*, with Moira Shearer as Ariel and John Gielgud as Prospero, but the project does not materialise.

Powell produces another play in London: *Hanging Judge* by Raymond Massey, based on a novel by Bruce Hamilton, with Godfrey Tearle. New Theatre from 23 September.

Alan Word's apologetic though informative biography, *Mr Rank* (London), provides a detailed account of the growth of the Rank organisation and its domination of British cinema.

1953   Twice Upon a Time

d/p—Emeric Pressburger. *p.c*—London Film Productions. *assoc. p*— George R Busby. *asst. d*—Sydney Streeter. *sc*—Emeric Pressburger, from Erich Kästner's novel *Das Doppelte Lottchen*. *ph*—Christopher Challis. *cam. op*—Freddie Francis. *a.d*—Arthur Lawson. *ed*—Reginald Beck. *m*—Johannes Brahms, Carl Maria von Weber. *m.d*—Frederic Lewis. *sd*—John Cox.

Hugh Williams (*James Turner*), Elizabeth Allan (*Carol-Anne Bailey*), Jack Hawkins (*Dr Matthews*), Yolande Larthe (*Carol Turner*), Charmaine Larthe (*Anne Bailey*), Violette Elvin (*Florence la Roche*), Isabel Dean (*Miss Burke*), Michael Gough (*Mr Lloyd*), Walter Fitzgerald (*Professor Reynolds*), Eileen Elton (*Ballet Dancer*), Kenneth Melville (*Ballet Dancer*), Nora Gordon (*Emma*), Isabel George (*Molly*), Cecily Walger (*Mrs Maybridge*), Molly Terraine (*Miss Wellington*), Martin Miller (*Eipeldauer*), Lily Kahn (*Mrs Eipeldauer*), Jean Stewart (*Mrs Jamieson*), Margaret Boyd (*Mrs Kinnaird*), Myrette Morven (*Miss Rupert*), Jack Lambert (*Mr Buchan*), Archie Duncan (*Doorman*).

75 mins. *t.s*—12 May. *GB rel*—6 July. *GB dist*—British Lion. *US rel*—floating 1953/4. *US dist*—Fine Arts Films.

'A story, told in flashback by the family doctor, of identical twins who meet by chance at a holiday camp in the Tyrol, discover that they are sisters — one lives in Glasgow with her mother, the other in London with her father — and bring together their divorced parents by changing identities. Their father, a well-known conductor and composer, is at the same time saved from the clutches of a designing ballerina.' (*Monthly Film Bulletin*). Another version of Kästner's novel was filmed in Germany in 1951.

1954 In June the government calls in the NFFC loan to British Lion and asks for a receiver to be appointed. Korda loses £500,000 of his own money, but manages to raise further finance privately and continues in production.

1955 At the invitation of Hein Heckroth, now working with the Frankfurt Opera, Powell agrees to direct a short film of a ballet *The Sorcerer's Apprentice*, to new music.

The Sorcerer's Apprentice

d—Michael Powell., *p.c*—20th Century-Fox/Norddeutscher Rundfunk. *p. designer*—Hein Heckroth. *solo dancer*—Sonia Arova. (no further credits available).

13 mins. (cut from c30 mins). *GB rel*—14 July. *GB dist*—20th Century Fox.

Oh Rosalinda!!

d/p/sc—Michael Powell, Emeric Pressburger. *p.c.*—Michael Powell, Emeric Pressburger. *assoc. p*—Sydney Streeter. *asst. d*—John Pellatt. *sc*—based on Johann Strauss' operetta *Die Fledermaus*. *lyrics*—Dennis Arundell. *ph*—Christopher Challis. *col*—Technicolor. *op*—Norman Warwick. *ed*—Reginald Mills. *p. designer*—Hein Heckroth. *assoc. a.d*—Arthur Lawson. *m*—Johann Strauss. *m.d*—Frederick Lewis. *choreo*—Alfred Rodriques.

Anthony Quayle (*General Orlovsky*), Anton Walbrook (*Dr Falke*), Dennis Price (*Major Frank*), Ludmilla Tcherina (*Rosalinda*), Michael Redgrave (*Colonel Eisenstein*), Mel Ferrer (*Captain Alfred*), Anneliese Rothenberger (*Adele*), Oska Sima (*Frosh*), Richard Marner (*Judge*), Nicholas Bruce (*Hotel Receptionist*). *The ladies:* Barbara Archer, Betty Ash, Joyce Blair, Hildy Christian, Pamela Foster, Jill Ireland, Patricia Garnett, Annette Gibson, Eileen Gourley, Jean Grayston, Grizelda Hervey, Maya Joumani, Olga Lowe, Sara Luzita, Ingrid Marshall, Alicia Massy-Beresford, Eileen Sands, Herta Seydel, Anna Steele, Jennifer Walmsley, Dorothy Whitney, Prudence Hyman.
The gentlemen: Michael Anthony, Igor Barczinsky, Cecil Bates, Richard Bennett, Nicholas Bruce, Ray Buckingham, Denis Carey, Rolf Carston, Terence Cooper, Robert Crewsdon, Peter Darrell, Edward Forsyth, Roger Cage, David Gilbert, Robert Harrold, Jan Lawski, Raymond Lloyd, William Martin, Kenneth Melville, Orest Orioff, Robert Ross, John Schlesinger, Frederick Schrecker, Maurice Metliss, Kenneth Smith, Richard Marner.
Voices of: Sari Barabas (*Rosalinda*), Alexander Young (*Alfred*), Dennis Dowling (*Frank*), Walter Berry (*Falke*).

101 mins. *t.s*—15 November. *GB rel*—2 January 1956. *GB dist*—Associated British-Pathe.

Powell: *Oh Rosalinda!!* got its awful title, I think, because it had been done in England as *Gay Rosalinda* — a popular version of *Die Fledermaus*. Nobody, certainly not ABC, would have let us call it *Die Fledermaus* and 'The Bat' is no good. It had some lovely things in it, but that again is one of our failures. By that time we were preparing and writing *Ondine* for Audrey Hepburn and Mel Ferrer, as well as *Battle of the River Plate.*'

1956 22 January, Alexander Korda dies.

The Battle of the River Plate

d/p/sc—Michael Powell, Emeric Pressburger. *p.c*—The Archers/J Arthur Rank. *assoc. p*—Sydney Streeter. *asst. d*—Charles Orme. *ph*—Christopher Challis (VistaVision). *col*—Technicolor. *cam. op*—Austin Dempster. *ed*—Reginald Mills. *p.designer*—Arthur Lawson. *assoc. a.d*—Donald Picton. *artistic adviser*—Hein Heckroth. *m*—Brian Easdale. *m.d*—Frederick Lewis. *sd*—C C Stevens, Gordon K McCallum.

John Gregson (*Captain Bell*), Anthony Quayle (*Commodore Harwood*), Peter Finch (*Captain Langsdorff*), Ian Hunter (*Captain Woodhouse*), Jack Gwillim (*Captain Parry*), Bernard Lee (*Captain Dove*), Lionel Murton (*Mike Fowler*), Anthony Bushell (*Mr Millington-Drake*), Peter Illing (*Dr Guani*), Michael Goodliffe (*Captain McCall*), Patrick McNee (*Lt Cmdr Medley*), John Chandos (*Dr Langmann*), Douglas Wilmer (*M Desmoulins*), William Squire (*Ray Martin*), Roger Delgado (*Captain Varela*), Andrew Cruickshank (*Captain Stubs*), Christopher Lee (*Manola*), Edward Atienza (*Pop*), April Olrich (*Dolores*).

119 mins. *t.s*—29 October. *GB rel*—24 December. *GB dist*—JARFID (Rank). *US rel*—November 1957 [106 mins]. US title — *Pursuit of the Graf Spee*. Royal Film Performance 1956.

Powell: 'Battle of the River Plate *was at the suggestion of Emeric. We had an invitation to go to the Mar Del Plata Festival in Argentina and it seemed a pity to go all that distance without a reason. He suggested a film about the* Graf Spee. *We looked up the contemporary accounts and talked to the Admiralty a bit and it seemed an absolutely fascinating story. So when we were there, we went to Montevideo and Buenos Aires and dug up quite a lot of people who knew about it, and we sold the idea to Spyros Skouras of Twentieth Century-Fox. We said that if he'd put up £5000 for writing a script, we'd do it.*'

Ill Met By Moonlight

d/p/sc—Michael Powell. *p.c*—The Archers/J Arthur Rank. *assoc. p*—Sydney Streeter. *asst. d*—Charles Orme. *sc*—based on the book of the same title by W Stanley Moss. *ph*—Christopher Challis (VistaVision). *cam. op*—Austin Dempster. *ed*—Arthur Stevens. *a.d*—Alex Vetchinsky. *m*—

Mikis Theodorakis. *m.d*—Frederick Lewis. *sd*—Charles Knott, Gordon K McCallum.

Dirk Bogarde (*Major Paddy Leigh-Fermor*), Marius Goring (*General Karl Kreipe*), David Oxley (*Captain Billy Stanley.Moss*), Cyril Cusack (*Sandy*), Laurence Payne (*Manoli*), Wolfe Morris (*George*), Michael Gough (*Andoni Zoidakis*), Roland Bartrop (*Micky Akoumianakis*), Brian Worth (*Stratis Saviolkis*), Paul Stassino (*Yani Katsias*), Adeed Assaly (*Zahari*), John Cairney (*Elias*), George Egeniou (*Charis Zògraphakis*), Demitri Andreas (*Nikko*), Theo Moreas (*Village Priest*), Takis Frangofinos (*Michali*).

104 mins. *t.s*—29 Jan 1957. *GB rel*—4 March 1957. *GB dist*—Rank. *US rel*—July 1958 93 mins US title—*Night Ambush*.

November: British and French invasion of Suez Canal zone.

1957 Powell publishes a book based on his researches for *The Battle of the River Plate: Graf Spee* (London).

Miracle in Soho

d—Julian Amyes. *p.c*—Rank Film Productions. *p*—Emeric Pressburger. *sc*—Emeric Pressburger. *ph*—Christopher Challis. *col*—Eastman Colour. *ed*—Arthur Stevens. *a.d*—Carmen Dillon. *m*—Brian Easdale. *sd*—Arthur Ridout.

John Gregson (*Michael Morgan*), Belinda Lee (*Julia Gozzi*), Cyril Cusack (*Sam Bishop*), Peter Illing (*Papa Gozzi*), Maria Burke (*Mrs Gozzi*), Rosalie Crutchley (*Mafalda Gozzi*), Ian Bannen (*Filippo Gozzi*), Barbara Archer (*Gwladys*), Billie Whitelaw (*Maggie*), John Carney (*Tom*).

98 mins. *t.s*—21 June. *GB rel*—4 August. *GB dist*—JARFID (Rank).

1958 Tony Richardson and John Osborne form Woodfall Films, linked to the English Stage Company and the Royal Court Theatre. Their first production is *Room at the Top*, directed by Jack Clayton.

1959 Luna de Miel (Honeymoon)

d—Michael Powell. *p.c*—Suevia Films-Cesario Gonsalez (Spain)/Everdene (GB). *p*—Cesario Gonsalez, Michael Powell. *assoc. p*—Sydney Streeter, Judith Coxhead, William J Paton. *p. sup*—Jaime Prades. *assoc. d*—Ricardo Blasco. *sc*—Michael Powell, Luis Escobar. *ph*—Georges Périnal (Technirama). *col*—Technicolor. *assoc. ph*—Gerry Turpin. *ed*—Peter Taylor, John V Smith. *a.d/cost*—Ivor Beddoes. *asst. a.d*—Eduardo Torre de la Fuente, Roberto Carpio, Judy Jordan. *m*—Mikis Theodorakis. *sd*—John Cox, Fernando Bernaldes, Janet Davidson.

Ballets: El Amor Brujo. *sc*—Gregorio Martinez Sierra. *m*—Manuel de Falla. *sets*—Rafael Durancamps. *choreo*—Antonio. *soloist*—Maria Clara

Alcala. *dancer*—Leonid Massine. *Los Amantes de Teruel. m*—Mikis Theodorakis. *cond*—Sir Thomas Beecham. *choreo*—Leonid Massine.

Anthony Steel (*Kit*), Ludmilla Tcherina (*Anna*), Antonio (*Himself*), Rosita Segovia (*Rosita*), Carmen Rojas, Maria Gamez, Diego Hurtado, Pepe Nieto.

109 mins. *France*—18 March 1961. *GB t.s*—31 Jan 1962 [90 mins]. *GB rel*—8 February 1962. *GB dist*—BLC. *Prize*—Special Prize of Commission Supérieure Technique, Cannes 1959.

Powell meets Leo Marks, a coding and cypher expert in government service, and they discuss a film on the life of Freud, but Huston announces a similar project (*Freud — The Secret Passion*, 1962). Instead Marks proposes a film 'about a boy who is warped by his father because he's got this bug about sound and vision and he uses the boy as a medical case.'

1960 Peeping Tom

d—Michael Powell. *p.c*—Michael Powell (Theatre). *p*—Michael Powell. *assoc. p*—Albert Fennell. *sc*—Leo Marks. *ph*—Otto Heller. *col*—Eastman Colour. *ed*—Noreen Ackland. *a.d*—Arthur Lawson. *m*—Brian Easdale, Wally Stott. *sd*—C C Stevens, Gordon K McCullum.

Carl Boehm (*Mark Lewis*), Anna Massey (*Helen*), Maxine Audley (*Mrs Stephens*), Moira Shearer (*Vivian*), Esmond Knight (*Arthur Baden*), Michael Goodliffe (*Don Jarvis*), Shirley Anne Field (*Diane Ashley*), Bartlett Mullins (*Mr Peters*), Jack Watson (*Inspector Gregg*), Nigel Davenport (*Sergeant Miller*), Pamela Green (*Milly*), Martin Miller (*Dr Rosen*), Brian Wallace (*Tony*), Brenda Bruce (*Dora*), Miles Malleson (*Elderly Gentleman*), Susan Travers (*Lorraine*), Maurice Durant (*Publicity Chief*), Brian Worth (*Assistant Director*), Veronica Hurst (*Miss Simpson*), Alan Rolfe (*Store Detective*), Michael Powell (*Mark's Father*), his son (*Mark as a child*).

109 mins. *t.s*—31 March. *GB rel*—16 May. *GB dist*—Anglo Amalgamated. *US rel*—15 May 1962 [86 mins]. *US dist*—Astor.

Powell: *'Peeping Tom* is a very tender film, a very nice one. Almost a romantic film. I was immediately fascinated by the idea: I felt very close to the hero, who is an "absolute" director, someone who approaches life like a director, who is conscious of and suffers from it. He is a technician of emotion. And I am someone who is thrilled by technique, always mentally editing the scene in front of me in the street, so I was able to share his anguish.' The film opens to a torrent of abuse in the press.

Hitchcock's *Psycho* opens in Britain at the end of August and provokes a further storm of indignation and disgust among reviewers.

Jean-Paul Török's review of *Peeping Tom* in *Positif* (translated here) is one of the first sympathetic studies of the film.

1961 The Queen's Guards

d/p—Michael Powell. *p.c*—Imperial. *assoc. p*—Simon Harcourt-Smith. *assoc. d*—Sydney Streeter. *sc*—Roger Milner, from an idea by Simon

Harcourt-Smith. *ph*—Gerry Turpin. *col*—Technicolor. *ed*—Noreen Ackland. *a.d*—Wilfred Shingleton. *m*—Brian Easdale. *sd*—James Shields.

Daniel Massey (*John Fellowes*), Robert Stephens (*Henry Wynne Walton*), Raymond Massey (*Captain Fellowes*), Ursula Jeans (*Mrs Fellowes*), Judith Stott (*Ruth*), Elizabeth Shepherd (*Susan*), Duncal Lamont (*Wilkes*), Peter Myers (*Gordon Davidson*), Ian Hunter (*Dobbie*), Jess Conrad (*Dankworth*), Patrick Connor (*Brewer*), William Young (*Williams*), Jack Allen (*Brigadier Cummings*), Jack Watling (*Captain Shergold*), Andrew Crawford (*Biggs*), Cornel Lucas (*Photographer*), Nigel Green (*Abu Sibdar*), René Cutforth (*Commentator*), Jack Watson (*Sergeant Johnson*), Laurence Payne (*Farinda*).

110 mins. *t.s*—9 October. *rel*—23 October. *dist*—20th Century Fox.

Emeric Pressburger publishes his first novel, *Killing a Mouse on Sunday* (London).

1963 Ian Johnson writes the first major article on *Peeping Tom* in English, 'A Pin to See the Peepshow', in an issue of *Motion* on sadism in the cinema.

Powell turns to television and directs the first of several one-hour films for long-running series.

Never Turn Your Back on a Friend (*Espionage* series)

d—Michael Powell. *p.c*—Herbert Brodkin Ltd. *exec. p*—Herbert Hirschman. *p*—George Justin. *assoc. p*—John Pellatt. *asst. d*—Bruce Sherman. *sc*—Mel Davenport. *ph*—Ken Hodges. *cam. op*—Herbert Smith. *ed*—John Victor Smith. *p. designer*—Wilfred Shingleton. *a.d*—Tony Woollard. *m*—Malcolm Arnold. *sd. rec*—David Bowen. *sd. ed*—Dennis Rogers. *titles*—Maurice Binder.

George Voskovek (*Professor Kuhn*), Donald Madden (*Anaconda*), Mark Eden (*Wicket*), Julian Glover (*Tovarich*), Pamela Brown (*Miss Jensen*).

48 mins. 1963.

Norway, during the Second World War. A three-man sabotage group, consisting of a Briton, a Russian and an American is controlled by the schoolteacher, Miss Jensen. After a raid on an installation they capture a German scientist who begs them to consult London about his importance: he is working on nuclear weapons. They are ordered to fly him out, but rivalry breaks out among the three and they kill each other, while the scientist catches his plane to London.

Dossier on *Peeping Tom* in *Midi-Minuit Fantastique* 8, including sequence breakdown, 'Les Mille Yeux du Dr Lewis' by Michael Caen, and an anthology of conflicting reviews.

1964 **A Free Agent** (*Espionage* series)

d—Michael Powell. *p.c*—Herbert Brodkin/MGM. *exec. p*—Herbert Hirschman. *p*—George Justin. *assoc. p*—John Pellatt. *asst. d*—Jake Wright.

sc—Leo Marks. *ph*—Geoffrey Faithfull. *cam. op*—Alan McCabe. *ed*—John Victor Smith. *p. designer*—Wilfred Shingleton. *a.d*—Anthony Woollard. *m*—Benjamin Frankel. *sd. rec*—Cyril Smith. *sd. ed*—Dennis Rogers.

Anthony Quayle (*Philip*), Sian Phillips (*Anna*), Norman Foster (*Max*), George Mikell (*Peter*), John Wood (*Douglas*), John Abineri (*Town Clerk*), Ernst Waldner (*Watch Factory Mechanic*), Gertan Klauber (*Innkeeper*), Vivienne Drummond (*Miss Weiss*).

48 mins. 1964

Two ex-secret agents, British and Russian, come to a small Swiss town to get married, although their former employers keep a close watch on them. It transpires that neither has resigned and both are following orders to marry the other. But Phillip's planned 'defection' to Moscow is prevented by Anna refusing to let him.

Bluebeard's Castle

d—Michael Powell. *p.c*—Norman Foster Productions/Süddeutscher Rundfunk. *p*—Norman Foster. *sc/m*—Bela Bartok's opera *Bluebeard's Castle. libretto*—Bela Balazs(1911). *ph*—Hannes Staudinger. *col.*—Technicolor. *p. designer*—Hein Heckroth.

Norman Foster (*Bluebeard*), Anna Raquel Sartre (*Judit*).

60 mins. Unreleased in GB.

Powell: '*Bluebeard's Castle* is merely a version of a one-hour opera pre-synchronised, recording the score first. We went to Zagreb and recorded the two singers with the Zagreb orchestra, and very good they were too. We edited the recording and then shot the film of it. A lot of it was, of course, Hein's decor, but those lovely shots of Foster seen through netting and gauze are very similar to what I do in other films. I have to admit it is very conscious.'

Pressburger's novel, *Killing a Mouse on Sunday*, is filmed as *Behold a Pale Horse;* directed by Fred Zinnemann, with Gregory Peck, Anthony Quinn and Omar Sharif.

1965 **The Sworn Twelve** (TV film for *The Defenders* series)

d—Michael Powell. *sc*—Edward DeBlasio *with* — E G Marshall, Murry Hamilton. King Donovan, Ruby Dee, Jerry Orbach. c50 mins.

An improperly influenced jury finds a defendent guilty of burglary.

A 39846 (TV film for *The Nurses* series)

d—Michael Powell. *sc*—George Bellak *with* — Michael Tolan, Shirl Conway, Joseph Campanella, Jean-Pierre Aumont, Kermit Murdock. c50 mins.

A physician who was tattooed with an identifying number in a concentration camp discovers a similar tattoo on an unidentified cadaver in a hospital.

Raymond Durgnat's article on Powell in *Movie* 14 (reprinted here) is the first large-scale study of his career and offers a reading in terms of Powell's relation to British cinema, culture and politics.

1966 They're a Weird Mob

d/p—Michael Powell. *p.c*—Williamson (Australia)/Powell (GB). *assoc. p*—John Pellatt. *asst. d*—Claude Watson. *sc*—Richard Imrie, from a novel by John O'Grady. *ph*—Arthur Grant. *col*—Eastman Colour. *ed*—G Turney-Smith. *a.d*—Dennis Gentle. *m*—Laurence Leonard, Alan Boustead. *m.d*—Laurence Leonard. *songs*—'Big Country', 'In this Man's Country' by Reen Devereaux; 'I kiss you, you kiss me' by Walter Chiari. *Cretan dance*—Mikis Theodorakis. *sd*—Don Saunders, Bill Creed.

Walter Chiari (*Nino Culotta*), Clare Dunne (*Kay Kelly*), Chips Rafferty (*Harry Kelly*), Alida Chelli (*Guiliana*), Ed Devereaux (*Joe*), Slim de Grey (*Pat*), John Meillon (*Dennis*), Charles Little (*Jimmy*), Anne Haddy (*Barmaid*), Jack Allen (*Fat Man in Bar*), Red Moore (*Texture Man*), Ray Hartley (*Newsboy*), Tony Bonner (*Lifesaver*), Alan Lander (*Charlie*), Judith Arthy (*Dixie*), Keith Petersen (*Drunk Man on Ferry*), Muriel Steinbeck (*Mrs Kelly*), Gloria Dawn (*Mrs Chapman*), Jeanne Dryman (*Betty*), Gita Rivera (*Maria*), Doreen Warburton (*Edie*), Barry Creyton, Noel Brophy, Graham Kennedy.

112 mins. *t.s*—7 October. *GB rel*—13 October. *GB dist*—Rank.

A young Italian journalist arrives in Sydney to work on his cousin's Italian-language newspaper, only to find that the cousin has taken off for Canada, leaving large debts. Nino starts to learn the language and repay the debts. Powell: 'That was merely a romp in Australia in the early American manner — like *Ruggles of Red Gap* for instance — except that I'm not such a good director of the human comedy as Leo McCarey. There are very few McCarey's, but it had the same quality generally and I was quite pleased with it.'

Emeric Pressburger publishes a second novel, *The Glass Pearls* (London).

1967 Powell co-produces an intelligence thriller based on a story by his former collaborator Leo Marks. *Sebastian* is directed by David Greene and stars Dirk Bogarde, Susannah York and John Gielgud. Released in April 1968.

1968 Bertrand Tavernier and Jacques Prayer interview Powell for *Midi-Minuit Fantastique* 20; the same issue also has Raymond Lefevre's *'Du voyeurisme à l'infini* on *Peeping Tom*. Thomas Elsaesser's review of *Tales of Hoffmann* appears in the first issue of *Brighton Film Review*.

Age of Consent

d—Michael Powell. *p.c*—Nautilus Productions (Australia). *p*—James Mason, Michael Powell. *assoc. p*—Michael Pate. *asst. d*—David Crocker. *sc*—Peter Yeldham, based on a novel by Norman Lindsay. *ph*—Hannes

Staudinger. *col*—Eastman Colour. *underwater ph*—Ron Taylor. *ed*—Anthony Buckley. *a.d*—Dennis Gentle. *m*—Stanley Myers. *sd*—Paul Ennis, Lloyd Colman.

James Mason (*Bradley Morahan*), Helen Mirren (*Cora*), Jack MacGowran (*Nat Kelly*), Neva Carr-Glyn (*Ma Ryan*), Antonia Katsaros (*Isabel Marley*), Michael Boddy (*Hendricks*), Harold Hopkins (*Ted Farrell*), Slim de Grey (*Cooley*), Max Moldrum (*TV Interviewer*), Frank Thring (*Godfrey*), Dora Hing (*Receptionist*), Clarissa Kaye (*Meg*), Judy McGrath (*Grace*), Lenore Katon (*Edna*), Diane Strachan (*Susie*), Roberta Grant (*Ivy*), Prince Nial (*Jasper*), Hudson Fausset (*New Yorker*), Peggy Cass (*New Yorker's Wife*), Eric Reuman (*Art Lover*), Tommy Hanlon Jr (*Levi-Strauss*), Geoff Cartwright (*Newsboy*).

98 mins. *GB rel*—15 November 1969. *US rel*—14 May 1969 [103 mins]. *dist*—Columbia.

Powell: 'The only failure of *Age of Consent* was that the artist himself was not original enough — I thought that let the film down.' While working with Mason, Powell discusses his project for *The Tempest* again.

1970 Raymond Durgnat's *A Mirror for England* (Faber, London) brings together previous writings on Powell and Pressburger and extends the discussion of their work in a study of 'British movies from austerity to affluence.'

July: death of Hein Heckroth in Frankfurt. Powell writes in *The Times*: 'Hein Heckroth has been an elder brother to me for more than 24 years, ever since we worked together on the ballet of *The Red Shoes* and on the design of the whole film. It was, I think, the first time that a painter had been given the chance to design a film, including the titles, and it was a triumph of work and organisation. For the ballet alone he made 600 sketches and they are preserved on film in the Museum of Modern Art, New York [and in the British Film Institute] . . . He was the sort of man who leaves an almost visible gap when he dies. He loved and understood youth. The other day he said to me: "Mickey, I understand what these kids are driving at. We should make money and buy guns to give to them, so that they can shoot us all".'

'Michael Powell' season at the National Film Theatre, London. Fourteen films are shown and a booklet, *Michael Powell: in collaboration with Emeric Pressburger*, (BFI, London n.d.) is edited by the organiser of the season, Kevin Gough-Yates. This booklet contains the long interview from which many of Powell's remarks on individual films given here are quoted; it also includes the only published interview with Pressburger.

1971 Powell gives a John Player Lecture during the NFT season under the title 'Beauty of Image' (10 January).

Roland Lacourbe publishes an exhaustive dossier, *'Introduction à l'oeuvre de Michael Powell'* in *Image et Son*.

1972 The Boy Who Turned Yellow

d—Michael Powell. p.c—Roger Cherrill. p. manager—Gus Angus. asst. d—Neil Vine-Miller. sc—Emeric Pressburger. ph —Christopher Challis. col—Eastman Colour. ed—Peter Boita. a.d—Bernard Sarron. m—Patrick Gowers, David Vorhaus. sd—Bob Jones, Ken Barber.

Mark Dightam (John), Robert Eddison (Nick), Helen Weir (Mrs Saunders), Brian Worth (Mr Saunders), Esmond Knight (Doctor), Laurence Carter (Schoolteacher), Patrick McAlinney (Supreme Beefeater), Lem Kitaj (Munro).

55 mins. GB rel—16 September. dist—Children's Film Foundation. Prize—Children's Film Foundation award, 'Chiffy', 1978.

1973 Interview with Powell by Richard Collins and Ian Christie in Monogram 3, a special issue on British cinema.

Powell tries again to find backing for The Tempest, with Mia Farrow as Ariel, and continues to develop various projects, including another children's film.

In A Heritage of Horror: the English Gothic Cinema 1946-72 (London), David Pirie discusses Peeping Tom as part of a 'Sadian' reaction against late 50s puritanism in Britain.

Powell retrospective at the Royal Belgian Film Archive, Brussels. A booklet is published containing a new interview and article by Kevin Gough-Yates and a filmography by Kingsley Canham (commissioned by the National Film Archive, London).

Painting by R B Kitaj, Kenneth Anger and Michael Powell, 96x60 ins.

1975 Powell publishes a novel set in Ireland. A Waiting Game (London).

Karol Kulik discusses Powell and Pressburger's relations with Korda in an extensively documented biography, Alexander Korda: The Man Who Could Work Miracles (London).

1977 Powell and Pressburger commissioned by Avon Books, New York, to write a novel based on The Red Shoes. Powell working on a film about the life of Pavlova as a Russian co-production.

1978 Pressburger attends first showing of The Life and Death of Colonel Blimp, newly reconstructed by the National Film Archive, at the FIAF Congress in Brighton.

Powell commissioned by BBC Television to shoot new material to

51

accompany television transmission of *The Edge of the World*. He produces *Return to the Edge of the World:* a prologue and epilogue to the original film, in which he and members of the original cast and crew re-visit Foula.

July: Powell receives the honorary degree of D Litt from the University of East Anglia.

October-November: a complete retrospective of the Powell-Pressburger collaboration, together with all extant films directed by Powell, at the National Film Theatre, London. The BFI publishes *Powell, Pressburger and Others* to coincide with this season.

2 Criticism

The Scandal of *Peeping Tom*

Ian Christie

The outraged press response to *Peeping Tom* on its release in 1960 has become a landmark in British cinema. Not only did it mark one of the decisive moments of unanimity among reviewers, a rare *prise de position*, but it virtually ended Michael Powell's career as a major director in Britain[1] and, in retrospect, it can be seen as inaugurating the era of naturalistic 'realism' that dominated the early 60s. My purpose in documenting and analysing this press dossier is not sociological (which would require consideration of the *institution* of press reviewing and its place in the cycle of production, distribution and consumption); nor is it merely to ridicule the reviewers of 1960 with the benefit of hindsight. On the contrary, the character of that near-unanimous response to *Peeping Tom* indicates that the reviewers accurately registered the *unacceptability* of the film when it appeared. Instead, I want to consider the affair as an intersection between the trajectory of Powell's 'deviant' cinema and the prevailing norms of British 'quality' cinema, both terms being inscribed in the discourse of the reviews. The basis for such a study has already been suggested by Charles Barr in a characteristically perceptive aside from his account of Ealing:[2]

> In British cinema [sexuality and violence] will . . . form a current running underground, surfacing only intermittently for instance . . . in the films of Michael Powell. Such work finds itself commonly written off as being in bad taste, a reaction which seems to indicate with equal frequency an embarrassment on the part of the films in dealing with such subject-matter and on the part of the critics in dealing with films that are *not* embarrassed by it: the latter applies more to Powell, the reception of whose films by English critics forms nearly as interesting a study as the films themselves.

'Sick . . . nasty . . . loathsome'

Before looking at the press reviews, it is perhaps worth noting that the 'trade' reviews of *Peeping Tom* were uniformly favourable and for the most part highly appreciative — at least of the film's commercial potential. The *Daily Cinema* rated it a 'compelling exploitation subject on title, theme and certificate', and went on to comment:

> It has an uncomfortable theme, yet one which is fraught with suspense. That

expert movie-maker Michael Powell has invested it with a maximum of technical excellence and all the quality of which he is capable . . . The horrific moments are not too many, since it is the theme itself which provides the emotional impact. (1.4.60)

Kinematograph Weekly found it 'thoughtful, as well as sensational', with the climax 'at once tender and horrifying'. (7.4.60). Like the other trade reviews, it praised Carl Boehm's performance as 'convincing and sensitive'. *Variety* took a more critical line, suggesting that Powell 'might have tightened up the story line', and objecting that Maxine Audley's part 'holds up the action to little purpose'; but its verdict was: 'saved from unpleasantness by shrewd direction and excellent photography. Above level horror pic.' (20.4.60).

The immediate background to *Peeping Tom* was of course the commercial success of the British horror film, especially the Hammer 'gothic' series, and the implacable hostility of most reviewers toward these[3]. Thus, for instance, the *New Statesman* (William Whitebait), which also introduces two of the subsidiary themes that run through the reviews: the reproach to Powell and the assertion of 'morbidity' in his earlier work.

> . . . *Peeping Tom* stinks more than anything else in British films since *The Stranglers of Bombay*. Of course, being the work of Michael Powell, it has its explanation, its excuse. But so had *The Stranglers*; it was 'history', you remember. *Peeping Tom* is 'psychology'. Why does the murderer with the cinematic itch and the skewering tripod do as he does? Because his father was a famous psychologist who specialised in Fear . . . But what worries me is that anyone at all could entertain this muck and give it commercial shape. The combination of the two is peculiarly nauseous; and it is odd to reflect that the last film of Mr Powell's we saw was *Battle of the River Plate*. True, before that, *A Canterbury Tale* and *A Matter of Life and Death* more than hinted at morbidity. (9.4.60)

These same themes are more elaborately orchestrated in *Tribune* (Derek Hill) in one of the most polemical reviews.

> The only really satisfactory way to dispose of *Peeping Tom* would be to shovel it up and flush it swiftly down the nearest sewer. Even then the stench would remain. Every now and then we're assured by industry representatives, the British Board of Film Censors, or some equally suspect authority that the boom in horror films is over. The truth is that there has been little if any decline in the number produced. It's merely that distributors are no longer prepared to put them before the critics. One can only assume that Anglo-Amalgamated were unusually proud of *Peeping Tom*, for their *Circus of Horrors* oozed into the London Pavilion a week later without any press show.
>
> *Peeping Tom* concerns a young film technician who kills girls by stabbing them through the throat with a sharpened leg of his tripod . . .

Other twists in the warped plot include the hero's spare-time pornographic photography, where his favourite model is a girl with a smashed lip; has romance with a girl whose first kiss prompts him to suck his camera lens turret; and his encounter with the girl's blind, drunken mother who reveals that the end of her stick is sharpened to match his own. (She also has the most memorable line: 'My instinct says all this filming isn't healthy.')

Obviously there's a legitimate place in the cinema for genuine psychological studies. But this crude, sensational exploitation merely aims at giving the bluntest of cheap thrills. It succeeds in being alternately dull and repellent.

It is no surprise that this is the work of Michael Powell, who displayed his vulgarity in such films as *A Matter of Life and Death, The Red Shoes* and *Tales of Hoffmann*, and the more bizarre tendencies of his curious mind in *A Canterbury Tale*, where the story consisted of Eric Portman pouring glue into girls' hair. In *Peeping Tom* his self-exposure goes even further. He not only plays the sadistic father, but uses his own child as his victim . . .

The immediate answer to trash like *Peeping Tom* is not more censorship, for that could only worsen a position rapidly growing impossible. The box-office is the real test — and not the West End box-office where anything that causes a stir in the press stands a chance of attracting a queue, but the provincial and suburban box-office. And that's where you come in — or rather, I hope, where you don't. (29.4.60)

Normally, some distinctions might be expected according to the target readership of the papers (middle-class/working-class; 'right'/'left'), but *Peeping Tom* seems to have cut across these boundaries and provoked a puritanical reaction from all sides. Thus *The Observer* (C. A. Lejeune) tries to 'retaliate' with a 'censorship' of the film:

> It's a long time since a film disgusted me as much as *Peeping Tom*. This so-called entertainment is directed by Michael Powell, who once made such distinguished films as *A Matter of Life and Death* and *49th Parallel*. The central character is a young photographer, who works in a film studio by day, and at night takes filthy pictures for profit and amusement. His father tortured him in childhood, and he has grown up as a pervert, a sadist and a murderer. His greatest pleasure is to skewer young women with the sharp leg of his camera tripod, and photograph the look of terror on their faces. Afterwards he relaxes in his snuggery, projects and gloats over the 'rushes' of their dying agonies. I don't propose to name the players in this beastly picture. (10.4.60)

The *Daily Worker* reviewer (Nina Hibbin) is so incensed that she fantasises a non-existent orchestral score (the music is entirely performed on piano):

> Obviously, Michael Powell made *Peeping Tom* in order to shock, In one sense he has succeeded.
>
> I was shocked to the core to find a director of his standing befouling the screen with such perverted nonsense.
>
> It wallows in the diseased urges of a homicidal pervert, and actually romanticises his pornographic brutality.

55

Sparing no tricks, it uses phoney cinema artifice and heavy orchestral music to whip up a debased atmosphere.

It even exploits the terror of a tormented child.

From its slumbering, mildly salacious beginning to its appallingly masochistic and depraved climax, it is wholly evil. (9.4.60)

Many of the reviews record similar responses, with the writers seeking extravagant and picturesque means of conveying their disgust. More interesting, are a group that try to identify to the specific concerns of the film. The *Daily Telegraph* (Campbell Dixon) alone focuses its review on *"voyeurisme'*:

The word for Michael Powell's *Peeping Tom* is, quite simply, nasty. Its concern is, fashionably, with *voyeurisme*, the central character being a young man who likes to kill women while recording their reactions during the process with a cine-camera . . .

So it goes on towards his own suicide, with telling touches of sadism, masochism, *voyeurism* and the rest, all of which appear to be evoked just for the hell of it. Altogether a work of great 'curiosity' as the book trade would say. Sick minds will be highly stimulated. (9.4.60)

David Robinson, who was responsible for both the *Financial Times* and the *Monthly Film Bulletin* reviews, enlarges on the theme of 'sadism' with a reference to the Marquis in the former and chapter and verse in the latter:

Any doubts that this is an authentically *Sadiste* films can be dispelled by a reference to the *120 Journees de Sodome*, especially Part IV, and the Murderous Passions numbers 41 and 46. It is only surprising that while the Marquis' books are still forbidden here after practically two centuries, it is possible, within the commercial industry, to produce films like *Peeping Tom*. De Sade at least veiled his enjoyment under the pretence of being a moralist. (MFB, May 1960)

Finally, in this group, the *Evening Standard* (Alexander Walker) reveals an engagement with the essential reflexivity of the film in a series of remarks scattered through an otherwise hostile review:

. . . a morbid desire to gaze is one of the commonest obsessions in life.

Unfortunately, Michael Powell's new film is just a clever but corrupt exercise in shock tactics which displays a nervous fascination with the perversion it illustrates . . .

. . . It exploits fears and inhibitions for the lowest motives. It trades in the self-same kind of obsession that it relates. (7.4.60)

Two other responses are worth noting as symptomatic of perceiving what issues the film raises and, simultaneously, seeking to repress this perception. The *News Chronicle* (Paul Dehn) effectively proposes a socially responsible 'revision' of *Peeping Tom*:

It is a fact that certain so-called *voyeurs* believe that they are too old or too ugly to be attractive to the target of their desires and so prefer diffidently and unselfishly to be onlookers rather than partakers.

This could be a valid and moving cinematic theme: but Mr Powell has brushed it commercially aside for the sake of ponderous, paper-backed horror. (8.4.60)

The other interesting realisation comes in *The Spectator* (Isobel Quigly), which begins by establishing that 'horror films are usually so crudely made that belief is never quite suspended'. Then, via regrets that 'a man who was once respected' should sink to this, to a comparison with Franju's *Les Yeux sans Visage*, reviewed shortly before, 'which I thought set a record for highbrow horrors'.

> . . . but it didn't involve you, it made little attempt at direct emotional realism, as *Peeping Tom* does; you had the creeps, but remotely, and often with amusement. *Peeping Tom* didn't make me want to streak out of the cinema shrieking, as Franju's film did at times; it gives me the creeps in retrospect, in my heart and mind more than in my eyes.
>
> We have had glossy horrors before (*The Fly*, for instance), but never such insinuating, under-the-skin horrors, and never quite such a bland effort to make it look as if this isn't for nuts but for normal homely filmgoers like you and me. (15.4.60)

Uniquely among the reviews, *The Spectator* (!) closes the circle, makes the vital connection, that *Peeping Tom* is a film for 'normal filmgoers', made within the despised genre of the 'British shocker', yet working against its normal transpositions (the Gothic world) to foreground precisely the 'unhealthiness' of 'all this filming'. Only *The Spectator* annotates the inscription of the normal/abnormal spectator.

Pleasure and Consumption

What is conspicuously absent from the reviews, in fact, is any sense of *recognition*. Not only is the 'matter' of the film held at arm's length as something nauseous, disgusting, essentially *dirty*; but the 'apparatus' is for the most part ignored. Although the reviews all mention Mark's nocturnal activities and his work at the film studio, they avoid following through the 'embedding' of the film process, whereby the apparatus of cinema is inscribed and re-inscribed in the body of the film, through a kind of Chinese-box structure. This phenomenon recalls the powerful taboos which surround the apparatus of cinema at all levels of the institution. Projectionists customarily guard against the danger of the audience seeing the 'blank' screen by opening the curtains while an image is being projected; and of course the injunction 'don't look at the camera' is axiomatic to conventional screen acting (and provides the title of British 'realist' filmmaker Harry Watt's autobiography). These taboos are often justified in terms of preserving the illusion, but it is not clear *which* illusion is being maintained. Could it be the security of *not being looked at?*

The basic reason for the non-recognition noted above is not hard to discover. It is a consequence of the dominant aesthetic in British cinema of uncriticial realism, which requires that any film be classified either as 'entertainment' (i.e. non-serious) or as a form of 'propaganda' (i.e. making a socially or personally ameliorative appeal). Since *Peeping Tom* offers a variety of 'pleasures' which cannot be enjoyed without acknowledging their origin in sadistic/masochistic drives — in other words, the 'normal' scopophilia of film consumption is inscribed and identified as the cause of the trouble — there is an automatic tendency to censor it. The reviews can be read, on one level, as a series of repressions, or attempts to censor the effectivity of the film, by assigning it to a category 'beneath contempt'. In this respect, *Tribune*'s instruction *not* to see it is particularly relevant. Equally interesting is the *Financial Times/MFB*'s indirect signposting by reference to the Marquis de Sade, whose writings were not then legally available in Britain (and here it is worth recalling the recent instances of the legal suppression of Pasolini's *Salo*, and the cultural intervention of the Film Work group's *Justine*, both reminders that de Sade still functions as a cultural token of 'the unacceptable').

What conclusions can be drawn from this brief anatomy of the press response to *Peeping Tom*? The criteria in play, the 'reading model' that the reviews propose, indeed impose, is a drearily familiar one. It rests upon a utilitarian aesthetic which, at one and the same time, divorces cinema from any effective involvement in the social formation, yet also seeks its justification in a 'relevance' to certain narrowly prescribed concerns — those of liberal humanism. This syndrome has been characterised by Don Macpherson:[4]

> . . . in neat antithesis to the idea of the passivity of unreflective consumption' is the premise that one of the qualities of art is that it makes you think'. This insidious type of intellectual appropriation succeeds in trying to isolate cinema, for example, from any suspicion of banality — that subjective' experience in which the I' is lost or forgotten in the stereotype of its response. Increasingly aestheticised, the cinema becomes a place to be made respectable by selection, a critics choice', rather than for an acknowledgement of the constant play on its fetishistic character which is the fascination' in the experience of the cinema.

The other term present in the reviews is a triumphant confirmation of the long-suspected 'morbidity' of Powell's work. The most frequently cited instance is the 'phantom glueman' of *A Canterbury Tale*, and item whose sadistic overtones seem to have lingered long in the memories of reviewers. Again it is *Tribune* that dissolves the issue into one of *vulgarity* — as opposed to subtlety/creativity/taste, etc. Within the consensus of British reviewing, the ultimate reproach to Powell (with or without Pressburger) is that he does not fit the canons of 'good taste'. To read the reviews down the years is to follow an oscillation between admiration and repulsion, a sustained ambivalence that becomes a standard discourse on Powell — 'on the one hand/on the other'. The point that is never grasped, and certainly not in the case of *Peeping Tom*, is that Powell operates precisely in the space between 'good' and 'bad taste'. What is active and dynamic in his work is the constant refusal to seek a justification other than in terms of what is possible in and through cinema.[5] Powell is the principle of cinematic specificity at work in British cinema; and the 'scandal' of *Peeping Tom* is the denial of that specificity, the refusal to acknowledge the illicit pleasure principle of cinema.

NOTES

1. Although he made the unsuccessful *Queens Guards* in 1961, Powell did not direct another feature until *The Boy Who Turned Yellow* for the Children's Film Foundation in 1971.

2. Charles Barr, *Ealing Studios* (London 1977), pp. 57-8.

3. The emergence of the Hammer cycle and critical responses to it, are well documented in David Pirie, *A Heritage of Horror* (London 1973).

4. Don Macpherson, 'Comments on *Marxism and Literature* (Raymond Williams)', *Edinburgh Magazine* 2, 1977, p70.

5. Powell admits as much in his interview with Tavernier and Prayer:
'. . . the majority of film makers of my generation have a style very much their own. Take Hitchcock for instance, or Renoir, these are film makers who have found their own style in the cinema. Not me, *I live cinema*. I chose the cinema when I was very young, sixteen years old, and from then on my memories virtually coincide with the history of the cinema. I have worked actively in the cinema for the last forty years and I live equally in the future, since I'm profoundly dissatisfied with what has been done so far. As I've already said, I'm not a director with a personal style, *I am simply cinema*. I have grown up with and through the cinema; everything that I've had in the way of education has been through the cinema; insofar as I'm interested in images, in books, in music, it's all due to the cinema.' (*Midi-Minuit Fantastique*, Oct 1968)

'Look at the Sea': *Peeping Tom*[1]

Jean-Paul Török

At the age of nine, Thomas Hardy, the greatest of English novelists, justly famed as a sensitive landscape painter of the southern counties, borrowed a nautical telescope and climbed the hill neighbouring his cottage to watch, in the pleasant town of Dorchester two miles away, the public hanging of a young woman. At the same age, Mark Lewis, the 'peeping tom' of Michael Powell's film, watches a couple making love while his father films his reactions with a hand-held camera. The father is an academic who has devoted his life to a study of the psychology of fear, using as a guinea-pig his own son, whose every emotion he photographs and records. In the middle of the night, camera in hand, he suddenly wakes the boy: he slips a lizard into his bed so as to capture the expression of naked fear and disgust on his face. Later he films him standing by his mother's death-bed. He keeps the child under constant observation, creating in him a voyeur psychosis that becomes identified in his mind with fear and the desire to cause suffering. Encouraged by his father, who presents him with a camera, the young Mark reacts against this threat that is poisoning his childhood by spying in his turn on the people around him. After his father's death, the young man continues his experiments, though not without adding certain refinements of his own, and no longer in a scientific spirit.

Sharing the common view that the cinema was invented in order to photograph the demise of pretty women in close-up, but preferring for the purpose a camera-knife in place of the less effective *caméra-stylo*, Mark Lewis perfects a very special 16mm camera: one of its feet, whose end unscrews, conceals a sharp-edged blade. Wielding this unsheathed sword horizontally in accompaniment to a final tracking shot, the cameraman plunges it into the victim's throat, keeping on filming her all the time, while a parabolic mirror clipped to the lens means that she, seeing her agony reflected, is provoked to a paroxysm of terror. This sequence as filmed by Powell achieves, if one thinks about it, a level of complexity as disturbing as the play of mirrors in a celebrated painting by Velazquez. The camera films the murderous film-maker, who films his victim, who observes the action first-hand as it unfolds. The spectator cannot but be favourably impressed by this death-watch on three planes.

But the purpose of *Peeping Tom* goes beyond these subtle games. It can be seen as a delicately nuanced psychological study of an authentic film *auteur*, who pushes a particular conception of the direction of actors to its limits. For voyeurism alone is not enough to explain the character of Lewis: he is also, and at one and the same time, a sadistic film-maker and murderer, with these different facets forming a coherent whole. A quite serious psychoanalytical explanation is adduced for this collection of morbidities, which will come as no surprise to those who know that in the look fixedly directed at someone, there lies an unconscious wish to cause suffering, and even to kill. One shoots with one's eyes and also, more effectively, with that substitute for the eyes, the camera. Surrounded by the police, Lewis, in place of the traditional machine-gun, turns his camera on them. One could go on citing examples: contrary to the old adage whereby we always kill the one we love — otherwise admirably illustrated by Belmondo killing a cop in *A Bout de Souffle* — Lewis refuses to film the girl he loves, and the only lover's promise he makes her is: 'I will never photograph you'. Worthy of note, too, is the care with which the sado-masochistic element in voyeurism is made explicit. Another English film has already offered for our delectation a pair of binoculars tricked out with two hidden steel spikes violently ejected by a spring into the eyeballs of anyone using them.[2] Here, by turning his camera on himself, Lewis ends by subjecting himself to the same treatment as he inflicted on his victims, completing his 'documentary' with an admirable close-up.

But who is the real voyeur? This pleasantly familiar title of 'peeping tom' also applies to the spectator, who is exceptionally privileged here: for is he not permitted to indulge that acme of voyeurism which consists in observing the voyeur, seeing what he sees and watching him watch? All the more so in that Powell's film is beautifully done. The fragments of 16 mm footage shot by Mark Lewis are edited and inserted into the action with great skill, so that the same sequence can be seen simultaneously from the point of view of the character observing it through his camera, and from the point of view of the director making the film.

Certain moments achieve a quite extraordinary sort of black poetry: the excerpts from the father's experimental films are bathed in the sheer light of terror, and the presence of the lizard in the child's bed is enough to tell us all that needs to be told about onanism and the castration complex. Thanks to skilful lighting effects, the murder in the studio is disturbingly effective. Lewis' final suicide, spectacular enough in itself, is accompanied by impressive funeral rites: police sirens, screaming children recorded on tape, flashbulbs exploding, cries of horror and assorted noises. As for the humour, it is cleverly used to enhance the moments of inaction. Lewis is in the street filming the police investigating his first murder: an inquisitive bystander asks what paper he is working for, and Lewis calmly responds by mentioning the very respectable British Sunday, *The Observer*. Similary, the old gentleman venturing into a sleazy shop to buy dirty pictures first asks for the *The Times*. And of course the only person to see clearly through this whole voyeur business is a blind woman.

At a time when the cinema currently in favour addresses itself exclusively to the intellect for admiration, it may seem beside the point to talk of the pleasure one feels in watching *Peeping Tom*. The extreme sophistication exercised by our modern film-makers in ringing the changes on their love play never cuts to the heart of the matter. In bed their characters behave like you and me. One likes occasionally to turn to other horizons, where dawns a more fantastic conception of eroticism. Photographing a largely unclothed woman in a dingy room, Lewis, in

---

[1]   Torok's remarkable early review anticipates the direction of much subsequent writing on/around *Peeping Tom*, both in France (*Midi-Minuit Fantastique*) and in Britain (*Motion*), although it remains unequalled.

[2]   *Horrors of the Black Museum* (Arthur Crabtree, 1959) with Michael Gough, June Cunningham, Shirley Ann Field. (Ed).

order to capture an unexpected expression of astonishment on her face, says to her: 'Look at the sea'. Good advice for scopophiliacs who are tired of the little birdies.

Translated by Tom Milne   *Positif No 36, 1960*

The Tales of Hoffmann

Thomas Elsaesser

Michael Powell is one of the few 'auteurs' that the British cinema has produced. His themes and preoccupations belong on the one hand to the best American tradition represented by such diverse masters as Welles, with whom he shares a keen eye for the mechanisms of power, manipulation and corruption, and Minnelli, whose concern with the artist in our society is likewise central to Powell. On the other hand, he also has affinities with the French cinema, notably with the Renoir of *La Carosse D'Or* ('where does the theatre end and where does life begin?'). And lastly, *Tales of Hoffmann* anticipates by more than a decade some of the formal and moral questions which Godard poses himself about the nature of the cinema in *Le Mépris*.

This is not to say that Powell is equal to any of these artists, but it might help to place him in a certain perspective. *Tales of Hoffmann* is no doubt seriously flawed, over-ambitious and uneven. It creates a confusing complexity, in which images of startling force are side by side with a rather too obtrusive, mechanical symbolism. But it is a film which is genuinely disturbing, not least by its uncompromising pessimism. Its importance derives from its partial failure: made in 1951, it foreshadows the decline of the great American cinema, and very accurately feels its way towards the modern 'continental' cinema, haunted as the latter is by an often paralyzing self-consciousness about the limits of the cinematic medium. Powell's unresolved formal problems stem directly from his themes, which seem to belong more to the 60s. The almost prophetic urgency of his themes has, as it were, wrecked the traditional narrative form and, today, one is inclined to view the fragments with singular affection and admiration.

The plot is most confusing, and at times quite impenetrable, but Powell's concern is clearly elsewhere. He has used his archetypal tale of romantic woes and sorrows to express by a complex *mise en scène* some of the important and provocative themes of modern society, in particular the dilemma of the cultural consumer, his inevitable alienation, and correspondingly, the artist in his dependence on the ruling class, corrupted and seduced, desperately fighting for his integrity. Two particularly striking images illustrate the dual theme: a satanic 'collector of souls' shapes the dripping wax of coloured candles into precious jewels as a lure for the courtesan to betray Hoffmann. The candle, traditional symbol of human life, is diabolically transformed into a false value to satisfy base instincts. The implication is that of a degraded art, corruptible and pliable as wax, in the hands of the modern magicians of culture. The other scene shows Hoffmann, after having defeated his rival and won the key, enter the courtesan's room. But he only finds a cage there. In his anger and disappointment over this discovery, he throws the key into the mirror which no longer reflects his image. The mirror cracks, and in the splinters Hoffmann once again beholds his own reflexion. Only after having broken the spell of a seductive world, does the artist regain his integrity, his reflexion.

Tales of Hoffmann, insofar as it is an account of the tragic relations between Hoffmann, the poet, and his creations, the three women who appear in his stories, is in a sense a pure meditation on the cinema, in its dual aspects of intimate art and mass-medium, of emotional reality and perverse illusion. Powell shows how the cinema is at once a means of artistic liberation (the magic spectacles of the optical inventor give Hoffmann a vision of unearthly beauty and love) and a tool of oppression (wearing the spectacles, Hoffmann is the victim of the puppet-master's deceptive game).

Powell makes very subtle use of the romantic archetypes in his material, by situating them in historical perspective. Some of the scenes are pure pastiches, tracing the decline and debasement of the romantic imagination during the later nineteenth and early twentieth centuries. (The gothic castle in the sea; the Venetian orgy with its decadent, pale noblemen; the monstrous Greek island of a fake neo-classicism; the flaming hearts and burning bushes of the Catholic revival). This method allows Powell a critique of his material, which is also a critique of the romantic cinema from German expressionism to modern horror-films, with a gamut of Mephistophelian characters, distinctly reminiscent of the Nosferatus, Draculas, Mabuses and Caligaris.

But these historical references are the more disturbingly effective, since the various guises underline and reinforce Powell's basic themes. Seen in this historical perspective, the analysis of the modern individual as a puppet dangling on strings which are pulled by many hands, gains an added poignancy. And it relates the protest of the imagination against this slavery and manipulation to the continual assertion of a fundamental and inalienable need for beauty and love, an assertion which is often as perverse as the slavery, and hopelessly self-destructive. (This bitter truth lies at the heart of another, often misunderstood work by Powell, *Peeping Tom*). In Powell's image of romanticism everything has become fiction and illusion, yet the particular tragedy of the modern world is that the forces of evil are now in command of the very means by which human beings have habitually protested against the miseries of their lives, namely the ability to seek refuge and consolation in the realms of beauty and love. Hoffmann is the victim of all these plots, because he is an artist, because he responds to beauty. His sensuousness is his most dangerous asset in a world where evil so freely manipulates the decor and stage-directs the heart. Powell, in his remarkable fable, shows how in our modern society we are robbed and destroyed by having our most precious and intimate needs debased. What makes us puppets of advertising and of all other forms of visual-sensual exploitation is precisely what in Powell's view, distinguishes us as still human: our capacity for emotional involvement and our need for beauty. Today, we lose both ways — in our real lives and in our dreams and fantasies.

Hoffmann is the reflexion of the spectator himself, visionary and victim at one and the same time. *Tales of Hoffmann* is the critique of the grand cinematic spectacle *à la Doctor Zhivago* in that it exposes the ideological insidiousness of the latter's commercial aestheticism.

But the true artist (and in this sense, Hoffmann is an image of Powell himself) is not afraid to run the risk of degradation and corruption; indeed, he has no choice but to commit himself to this debased world if he wants to remain an artist. Even the courtesan is moved by Hoffmann's song, and the puppet is touched by his love, responding to it with a troubled flutter of her mechanical eyes, which seems to break the spell of her soulless being under the magic of the poet's tenderness. Hoffmann is a modern Orpheus, bringing new life to the inanimate and corrupt.

Yet he is the victim of a specifically modern world, exploited by the diabolic ingenuity and unholy alliance of technology (the optical inventor) and managerial salesmanship (the puppet master and his acolytes), robbed of his reflexion (in the mirror) by the embrace of the courtesan, symbol of material riches (the waxen jewels) and a dark troubled sensuality (her image rising from the rippling water of the Venetian lagoon), and finally cheated of his true love by the immorality of science (the diabolic doctor) and mad ambition (the girl's father). As a modern Orpheus, Hoffmann's love has a redeeming quality, it is both life-giver and protest against a cold world of manipulation, greed, and domination. But it is a redemption that saves neither his beloved nor himself.

The nihilism of Powell's film is so thorough and relentless that it forces him into a desperate aestheticism, where the only moral stance is the hopeless affirmation of a doomed innocence, born from too much knowledge and self-awareness about the evils of our world. One can see why Powell was attracted by the material, which itself is Offenbach's interpretation of tales by the romantic poet E. T. A. Hoffmann. The three different media — literature, music and the cinema interpret each other as successive stages of a cultural critique, as the historical modes of experiencing and expressing the same nihilistic despair.

Powell belongs to the modern Romantics, and in his tragic aestheticism he is very like Godard in his early films (until *Pierrot Le Fou*) — both are reactionary Romantics, whose protest against the modern world is the acceptance of death, indeed of suicide, as the inevitable price to be paid for remaining an artist, and therefore, human.

Brighton Film Review No 1, 1968

1.   See also, Thomas Elsesser's introduction to *Monogram* 3 on British Cinema, 'Between Style and Ideology'.

Durgnat on Powell and Pressburger

Raymond Durgnat is the only British critic who has written extensively on Powell and Pressburger, and consistently recognised their importance in any 'dialectical' history of British cinema. His 1965 auteur *article (originally published in* Movie *under the pseudonym 'O O Green', and here slightly revised) was the earliest attempt to assess their significance and analyse it. The issues raised in this essay were subsequently developed in Durgnat's* A Mirror for England *(1970); and are re-considered in the following essay on* The Small Back Room, *specially written for this book.*

Michael Powell

For some time now Michael Powell has been fashionably dismissed by critics as a 'technicians' director', a virtuoso of the special effect, with a joltingly uneven storysense, for whom, indeed, a narrative was only an invisible thread permitting the startling juxtaposition of visual beads. To observers of the simplistic distinction between 'style' and 'content', he seemed a stylist and a rhetorician, camouflaging an absence of idea by a weakness for the grandiose, out-of-context effect.

There is indeed a sense in which he can be described as Britain's answer to Abel Gance (and it won't be very long before he, too, has his NFT season). Both directors have a weakness for patriotic sentiment (Powell's more veiled than Gance's), both have a weakness for optical shocks. (Gance's 'the camera becomes a snowball' could be paraphrased by 'the camera becomes an eyeball', when the pink-and-mauve eyelid-lining closes over the screen in *A Matter of Life and Death*). And both seek to ornament *melodrama* by visual style rather than by re-thinking the *drama*.

The myth of Powell as a 'mindless eye' overlooks explicit ideological positions like the High Tory moral of *A Matter of Life and Death*. The film then ceases to be an assemblage of technical effects and metaphysical tags: whatever its weaknesses (which themselves indicate the spirit of its time and class) it has a consistent theme and 'body', and its various episodes and ingredients appear as spokes radiating from a central hub. An inability to think in terms of 'content' must be attributed, not to Powell, but to his critics, who didn't see that the film was as political as *The Life and Death of Colonel Blimp*. It's ironic that the fiercest attack on the film (as decadent, sadistic, Fascist, and what-have-you) came, not from left-wing critics, who didn't even see that it was an anti-Socialist film, but from E. W. and M. M. Robson, whose ideological position was not far from Powell's own.

But though 'High Tory' morals and atmospheres are clearly discernible in other Powell films such as *I Know Where I'm Going*, and *The Queen's Guards*, our concern here is not with any similarities between Michael and Enoch. Indeed, the heroine of *I Know Where I'm Going* renounces the materialistic marriage offered her by the tycoon, to embrace values more traditional, more rural, more spiritual, and more mysterious. The director's 'typical hero' is a 'country gentleman'; he takes a romantic view of the military life; and, as Richard Winnington remarked at the time of its release, the basic idea of *A Canterbury Tale* was 'to endow an accidental wartime excursion to Canterbury with the hushed, bated magic of Pilgrim's Way, to link in mystic suggestion the past and the present ...'

'In mystic suggestion . . .' It would be a pity if the political interpretation, however correct, of Powell's films obscured another source of his inspiration, a source whose mixture of strengths and weaknesses is the subject of this article — an article making no claim to be the exhaustive survey which his work deserves.

For, if Michael Powell is an 'eccentric technician', it is in the sense of that proverbially English phenomenon, an eccentric Colonel. When stiff-upper-lip Colonels retire from such matter-of-fact activities as strategy and gunnery, they proverbially embrace strange, soggy systems of mystical belief. This type of hard-edged soft-centred-mysticism is not exclusively English and commoner than one might think: Doris Lessing described her father's in *In Pursuit of the English*; the Amberson family patriarch is another specimen, and so is General de Gaulle. Similarly, when the brilliant technician Powell leaves off, there begins a man who dabbles in mysticisms and romantic emotions of every kind: not only the 'Kiplingism' of his English officers and countryside, but in his fables for the Celtic fringe (*The Edge of the World, I Know Where I'm Going, Gone to Earth*), in pagan spiritual forces repelling Christian nuns from Himalayan peaks in *Black Narcissus*, in the fate-time warp of *A Matter of*

Life and Death, in the hothouse world of opera-ballet (*The Red Shoes, Tales of Hoffmann, Oh Rosalinda!, Honeymoon*), in the hallucinated soul (*The Small Back Room, Peeping Tom*).

Indeed, the adaptation of Nigel Balchin's novel illustrates his penchant for opening up the romantic veins of his 'sober' subjects, by blossoming into an (ill-advised) expressionist sequence as David Farrar, in the grip of theDTs, sees himself trying to scramble up the sheer smooth sides of a Kong-sized whisky bottle. The most powerful passage in *The Battle of the River Plate* is the camera's chilling inspection of the battleship's grey, silent mass, a vast, complex killing city, a technological Moby Dick, conspicuously invested with a Satanic nobility. And its naval battles catch, visually, the gaudy fervours of the battle paintings in regimental messes. Powell's interest in technological devices enables him to transpose into contemporary terms this underlying romanticism. The veteran officer of *The Queen's Guards* hauls his crippled frame about the room on a complex rig-cum-cradle. Peeping Tom's movie-camera has two very optional extras: the front leg of the tripod conceals a blade with which he bayonets sufficiently beautiful subjects, and, as he photographs their dying agonies, a distorting mirror replacing the reflector enables them to share the show, and re-infect them with their own fear, squared. *Cinéma-vérité* cuts to the quick . . . Here Powell's sense of apparatus attains a convulsive poetry.

Somehow, Powell seems born into the wrong period. Had he, and the cinema, and Technicolor, been born during any of the periods celebrated in Mario Praz's *The Romantic Agony*, he might have been working with the cultural grain instead of against it. Admittedly his 'romantic-expressionist' films chime in with a post-war English nostalgia for period exoticism. The multi-millionaire (Eric Portman) of Terence Young's *Corridor of Mirrors* openly felt he was born in the wrong century and built Renaissance Venice in his grounds to prove it. Thorold Dickinson's *The Queen of Spades*, Michael Relph and Basil Dearden's *Saraband for Dead Lovers*, Lean's Dickenses, Korda's *An Ideal Husband* and Olivier's Shakespeare, all register this middlebrow escapism from '40s austerity. But Powell's craving is more audacious, more interesting, more constant, more uncertain, as he turns this way and that, restlessly seeking out different genres, styles, symbols.

Its (Tory) political overtones apart, *I Know Where I'm Going* asserts the antagonism of the orderly, money-based world of the heroine (Wendy Hiller) to the irrational but wise worldliness of Celtic myth. Paganism overwhelms Christianity — the heroine tries to say her usual prayers, but the real occult force is making a wish while counting the roofbeams of the eerie cottage. The bluestocking heroine's Shavian brashness about money is queered by wayward Celtic winds-and-waves. She is worked upon by a group of Celtic females (Pamela Brown, Sybil Thorndike) whose 'wisdom' is disturbing rather than reassuring. They have the glances of eagles — indeed, the hero (Roger Livesey) has an eagle's nose and an elderly 'Major' is training a golden eagle which bears the young man's name. Altogether the film neatly, nicely dovetails the 'magic' world with that of ration books and faulty telephone-cabins, maintaining a nice ambiguity — the curious British blend of knowledge that the romantic-occult isn't true, with a wish to believe that somehow it might be. Only at one point is the Celtic myth debased to the domesticated whimsy of middle-class romanticism. The young laird finally braves a family curse forbidding him from entering his ancestors' keep — and finds the curse was actually a challenge, ambiguously concealing from all but the first to defy it a liberation from its reputation. A legend about lovers chained together to drown 'parallels' a modern story about lovers being 'chained' together in marriage. Maybe Powell intends to stress that country gentry Toryism mustn't be too traditional, must continue tradition by defying it, and be more like brain surgeons than Blimps: all three characters, incidentally, are played by Roger Livesey. One might suspect that Powell is merely exploiting the myths to provide a little 'local colour'. But if he disbelieves the specific myths, his fondness for myth reveals a serious belief in the wayward natural forces which myths maintain against our too-tidy reason. He has never quite managed to bring their full power into his films. There are constantly hints, jabs of it: a close-up of the eagle tearing a rabbit's ear off; nature, for Powell, is not just an inspirational calendar, but also a Nietzschean whirl of blood and death. The heroine bribes a foolish young boatman to defy the storm; but the hero sails the boat through the treacherous whirlpool, overcoming those forces with a protective manliness, which, like that of the Hebridean islanders who dwell on *The Edge of the World*, is itself a force of wild nature. Even the defensive comic relief about Tory-Celtic 'eccentricity' had a sharpness of its own — as the women kiss their kin on the mouth, as the peppery old eagle-trainer dodders about with a featherduster and a hairnet, looking mildly like Oliver Hardy in drag, and calling the hero 'potty' for considering marriage.

Less dated than *Brief Encounter*, *I Know Where I'm Going* isn't dissimilar in theme and tone. Its story enables Powell to integrate his somewhat centrifugal qualities in a way which doesn't recur until *Peeping Tom*.

In each film of Powell's, this romantic urge sports a different livery — co-existing with the everyday and with an only mildly pusillanimous humour (the Heavenly Messenger is always heralded by the smell of fried onions). Its recurrent forms are political toryism ('Country Gentry Freedom Works'), professional soldiering (especially our gallant Prussian foes[1]), and ballet-opera — suggesting that it is these forms that seem to Powell to survive the hardheaded tests which he does in fact apply. His central problem as an artist has been his tendency to fall between the two stools of romanticism and realism, to 'escape from' (or schematise) the latter, yet only 'play with' the former. The two aspects of his vision remain flawed and, as it were, unconvinced — leading to a third besetting vice, a summary way with human emotion. Romantic in potentiality is his daring way with technical effects — a huge Technicolor close-up of an eyelid closing, seen from within, or the camera panning to and fro with a ping-pong ball until Time stops and players and balls stand transfixed. Yet, all too often, the technical fireworks are frittered on merely decorative details: in *The Elusive Pimpernel* abstract patterns appear, but only to give us visual equivalent of a sneeze. And yet Powell never deigns to give such patterns a deeper pretext and add 'abstract expressionism' to his repertoire of artistic effects.

His weaknesses are displayed in his four ventures into opera-ballet. *The Red Shoes* revived the Rouben Mamoulian tradition. Banal in its view of ballet-life, schematic in its romantic view of art as that blend of the sublime and the diabolical which Bergman propounded with vastly greater sophistication and force in *Summer Interlude* and *The Face, The Red Shoes* has suffered the fate usually endured by works of art which, otherwise inspired, show a new stylistic flexibility (in colour palette); instantly overpraised they appear infuriatingly pretentious for years afterward before finding their own level — an honourable one. It survives for some lyrically coloured scenes and for a climactic ballet which, despite some ugh touches perpetrated by Powell's notoriously erratic taste, blends, by and large, an effective simplicity *à la* Kelly-Donen with an expressionism which was Powell's and Heckroth's own — drifting pieces of sad, sickly cellophane suggesting gaiety's futility, some sharp colour discords.

It is to Powell's credit that, seemingly bored with this simplicity, he banked everything on all-stops-out expressionistic clutter for *Tales of Hoffmann*. This gallimaufry of Gothicisms, this pantechnicon of palettical paroxysms, this meddle-muddle of media, this olla podrida of oddsbodikins, this massive accumulation of mighty midcult Wurlitzerisms, follows Offenbach's operetta faithfully and fills in filmically with ballet, decor and by-play, seeking, moreover, an operating visual style with a total disdain of plausibility. The artists have turned their back on current 'interpretative' fashions and sought to recapture the fullblown romantic surge.

To object to the overloading, to the clutter *per se,* is like objecting to the 'thickness' of Keats, of Poe. It cocktails up many of nineteenth century romanticism's idioms: the Greek, the Gothic, Balzacian courtesans, doppelgangers, the devil, sexual oddities (Pamela Brown in drag), and, over and over, art as diabolical. It's not courage this film lacks; it's taste, in the sense of economy of means; it's ugly, in an inexpressive way, ugly even when the theme requires beauty. One need only compare the awkward way in which human and puppets are mixed in a quadrille with the similar mixture in the nighclub scene in Marcel L'Herbier's *La Nuit Fantastique,* a film made by an academic who, however, had grown up within a climate infected by Surrealism, by the sombre, toughly Marxist poetry of Prévert-Carné, by Delluc, by Vigo. Powell-Heckroth have as inspirational heritage and trampoline the visual culture of Ye Olde Junke Shoppe.

Unreservedly successful are those sequences whose embellishments are photographic rather than architectural — Moira Shearer in dragonfly tights, photographed through a smudged green filter; or a split screen showing four elevations of Moira Shearer in white with a black-cloaked porteur who emerges into a black background. Though frequently overblown to the point of gruesomeness, the film is incessantly breathtaking, an effect which survives repeated viewings; perhaps, after all, it's a bad taste classic, and the predominant word there is 'classic'; in his autobiography Joseph von Sternberg pays a generous tribute to the haunting quality of its visuals.

The next film in the series, *Oh, Rosalinda!* is a four-power *Fledermaus*, a weird and, to my mind, rather wet blend of opera-bouffe and topical satire, with The Bat topically metamorphosed into a sort of Harry Lime of love. Powell lovingly adds absurdities of his own to the operatic convention — a duet sung over the telephone is interspersed with short snatches of dance. Made relatively cheaply (the sets are painted rather than built) it oddly misuses its high-voltage battery of talent — Michael Redgrave has more dancing to do than Ludmilla Tcherina. As for *Honeymoon*, which floated into only a few cinemas here, despite its inclusion of La Tcherina's stunning 'total-theatre' type ballet, *Les Amants de Terual*, criticism cannot speak fairly of a film so hacked by its distributors. Since then Powell has abandoned the field of filmed opera-ballet.

Black Narcissus, The Elusive Pimpernel and *Gone to Earth* represent Powell's Lyceum streak. The first contrasts the Anglican nuns (Mother Superiored by Deborah Kerr) in their lofty Tibetan convent whose spiritual serenity is rudely disrupted by the Himalayan heights, by local superstitions, by the silent and immovable 'holy man' whose superhuman asceticism shames them, by the cynical Oriental wisdom of the local ruler (Esmond Knight), by the earthy physicality of David Farrar, who rides on a donkey with his hairy, sexy legs dangling, and typifies *l'homme moyen sensuel*, by homesickness, by jewel-in-nosed dancing girl Jean Simmons, symbolising Oriental sensuality, and by Kathleen Byron as the sex-maddened sister who, trying to murder the Mother Superior, only falls to her death in her sinful scarlet dress from the very bell which dared challenge the sullen, deep tone of the Tibetan mountain-horns. Alas, not even Jack Cardiff's glittering colour photography of Jean Simmons' tawny-and-green eyes can redeem Rumer Godden's story from its fatal defect (shared by *The Greengage Summer*), a clumsy chopping-to-and-fro between a basically 'naice' idea of English life, a tourist's idea of the exotic, and screaming-and-strangling melodrama.

Similarly, *The Elusive Pimpernel* is sapped by the naivety of the Baroness Orczy elements, which P and P accept but endeavour to camouflage by their pictorial virtuosity — quite 'hand-held' in its effect is a dazzling game of Blind Man's Bluff where the aristocratic ladies blindfolded George III with a black scarf from under one corner of which he and we can see a whirling circle of sumptuously creamy bosoms.

Attempts are made to liven up that stock and static scene where a lady alone at her dressing table receives and reads an important note — here, she finds it on the floor and stretches herself out at full-length in order to read it. Powell has certainly escaped the visual stuffiness of Korda's *Lady Hamilton*. But why take Orczyism on its own terms in the period of Burt Lancaster, Kirk Douglas and Robert Mitchum?

As a result of Korda's hook-up with Selznick, P and P find themselves struggling with sultry passion in *Gone to Earth* (or *The Wild Heart* in the USA and on British TV), with Jennifer Jones as Shropshire's answer to Pearl Chavez. *Duel in the Sun* is a bad taste masterpiece which is also a good taste masterpiece, for its vulgarity is that of its conviction. Throughout the British film, the American star seems *yearning* for someone to make a passionate film round her, to whirl her into it. From King Vidor's film she remembers, postures, gestures. But Powell, stilted or shy, like so many compatriots of his generation, in the presence of erotic intensity, fears embarrassment and ridicule, cuts away to 'local colour' (harpists, landscapes) and *faux-naif* cliché (the bad squire's black boot stamps on the girl's rosy posy). Powell's respect for unfashionable *genres* is in itself admirable but so often he accepts what is worst rather than what is best in them. A schematic colour symbolism proves thin compensation for dramatic hollowness; the red of the huntsman contrasts with the black of the churchgoing middle-groups, both groups being concerned, in their different ways, to hunt down the fey fox heroine. The result is neither Selznick nor Mary Webb — for romanticism is passion creating its own universe, or it is nothing.

The recent deluge of Technicolor horror might have offered Powell a congenial climate for his lyrical propensities; and it's characteristic of his ever-astonishing mixture of gifts that his near-miss to a masterpiece, *Peeping Tom*, is a very different kettle of fishiness. The storyline is excessive enough to carry almost any amount of dramatic weakness, and still be breathtaking; in a scnsc, it nccds a 'cool' style, for the Peeping Tom camcraman (Carl Boehm) is secretive, passionless, lonely. As appropriate to a study in repressions and inhibitions, the film is built on symbols and references, which have been admirably schematised by Ian Johnson.[2] The eye-mirror-camera motif recalls the brain surgcon with his *camera obscura* in *A Matter of Life and Death* (another 'cutting *voyeur*'), and reminds us that P & P's trademark as 'The Archers' was a close-up of an arrow smacking into a bull's *eye*. Little need to dwell on the erectility of the bayonet-tripod, while Mark Lewis's job as a *focus-puller* underlines the *voyeur*'s association of seeing with sexual protuberance. The old woman who 'sees through' the quiet young man to his real nastiness is blind. (Indeed, she's related to the Celtic women with their 'second sight'; for Anna Massey, playing her daughter, looks like Pamela Brown in *I Know Where I'm Going*.) Mark has his tripod, the old woman has her stick. He has his mirrors, she has her wisdom. The Oedipal situation is lovingly elaborated. Mark paraphrases on his 'models' the experiments his father, a world-famous psychologist, inflicted on him — experiments on the effect of fear — throwing a lizard (cold-eyed phallic 'snake') onto his bed, shining a bright light into his eyes, showing him his own films. Mark has kept his father's films of the experiments: also shots taken by his father of his stepmother, a bosomy young thing whom he married six weeks after Mark's mother's death and who looks like the nude models whom Mark earned pocket-money by photographing (Pamela Green and the girl with the disfigured lip). The film abounds in films-within-films (opening with Mark's new film of a murder, and taking in its stride both the film on which Mark is working at the studio and Mark's father's films of young Mark). The film's plethora of in-jokes out-Cahiers *Cahiers*. Mark's father is played by Michael Powell; the director of the feature film is played by Esmond Knight, who is blind; the hero is called Mark Lewis, presumably after the scriptwriter, who is Leo Marks; the Esmond Knight character is called Arthur Baden, Baden-*Powell* being the man who looks after little boys and trained their characters. Mark gets involved mainly with red-headed women — most Powell heroines are redheads too — Mark describes himself as a correspondent from *The Observer* and his father tells him to 'Look at the sea' — 'Look at the see' being what his victims do in the *mirror* which replaces the *reflector*. The black-and-white flashbacks to 'clinical' child-torture relate to the coloured present in a way reminiscent of Resnais' *Nuit et Brouillard*. The film is built on refusing to allow the audience to hate the torturer, on a cold hysteria of frustrated indignation, stoked up by such a sacrilegious idea as casting Moira Shearer as a bitch, fit fodder for a sensitive sex murderer. In the last split-second, Mark, in a dying hallucination, is reconciled with his long-dead father. Here art reveals, again, its diabolic root, and reconciliation with the diabolic is an underlying *leitmotif* in Powell — in the close association between the gallant Prussian soldier and the Nazi cause, in the cruel paganism of *I Know Where I'm Going*. The hero, there, subdues nature, or rather survives it, because he has nature's intensity. Indeed, Powell has a fondness for leading men with a certain sharp, hard intensity about them — Roger Livesey, Marius Goring, Anton Walbrook, and, in a different modality, David Farrar, just as his women are often half-witches. Yet, ironically, the one film in which he needed to explore emotional intensity in depth — *Peeping Tom* — depends on what is, in effect, the deadpan pleasantness of Carl Boehm, and the dimension therefore lacking is more vividly asserted in *Repulsion*, by the confluence of Catherine Deneuve's nervous tension and Roman Polanski's eye for the eerie. In this game of hide-and-seek between the inhibited and the diabolical, the patriotic and the exotic, the traditional and technological, the Tory and the pagan, Powell's work finds much of its fascination and its disquiet.

His two most satisfying films are, perhaps, *Peeping Tom* and the child's Arabian Nights fantasy *The Thief of Bagdad* (1940), for which he shares directorial credit with Ludwig Berger (German specialist in trick-and-costume films) and Tim Whelan (an efficient Hollywood craftsman). This too carries many distinctly Powellian notations — almost its first shot is of a painted eye on a boat's prow, surging up into close-up, its story (by Miles Malleson) includes the theft of the all-seeing eye (*Peeping Tom!*) from a Tibetan temple (*Black Narcissus!*); the giant genie from the bottle (beautifully incarnated by Rex Ingram, who played God the Father in *Green Pastures*) prefigures the gigantic bottle in *The Small Back Room;* its tricks with fate-and-time parallel *A Matter of Life and Death.* If it never quite transcends the sphere of children's film to become an adult's fantasy too, it remains one of the classic screen fantasies, surpassing Roy Rowland's *The 5000 Fingers of Dr. T* and Joseph Von Baky's *The Incredible Adventures of Baron Munchausen*; its scope and audacity, its morning freshness, reduce Cottafavi's *Hercules Conquers Atlantis* to small beer. It's characteristic of the Powell paradox that his two best films should be an epic for grown-up children and a very queasy study of a tormented childhood.

Whence this contrast, this centrifugality? The comparison with King Vidor is pertinent. Vidor, intellectually, perhaps, less sophisticated, or at least less cautious, than Powell, has retained just that Wagnerian authenticity of emotional excess which gives his films that genuine mysticism, their quality of that strange thing, a Nietschzean pantheism. But Powell lived in a class and a country which suspects, undermines, is embarrassed by, emotion; his diversity of qualities rarely find their holding context. Between himself and Hoffmann he interposes the opera-ballet convention; whereas the (American) Corman-Crosby team, in their horror films, blend Poe, Wilde, Freud and colour expressionism into a coherent universe. It would not be altogether unreasonable to see Powell's directness as the Pirandellism of scepticism, to see Powell's ballet films as preludes to an *8½* which he hadn't the egotism to make. One would dearly like to see him tackle those science-fiction subjects which have a built-in excess — C. E. Moore's 'Shambleau', Richard Matheson's 'I Am Legend', Damon Knight's 'The Analogue Men'. And he is the only director who could bring to the screen *Fleming's* James Bond.

He remains an upholder, through its lean years, of the Méliès tradition. His films shed not a little light on English thought and the English soul, in its restraints, its pussilanimity, its nostalgia for a German expressionsism, its coy amorality. But their authenticity, in terms of some conventionalised realism, isn't the only criterion; at their very flimsiest, they still engross and reward one's attention, they give pleasure by half-belonging to *our* world and half to their own. They relate to a still-ill-defined tradition of, not so much decorative cinema, as extravaganza-formalism, like the Nazimova *Salome* and the Max Reinhardt *A Midsummer Night's Dream* — to a spectacular cinema which asks the audience to relish the spectacle *as such*, to a school of 'Cinema' which is always exquisitely conscious of, not only its cinematic effects but its cinematic *nature*. And thus it rejoins, by its own route, the minimalist-formalism of subsequent avant-gardes.

Movie No 14, 1965

1   In *The Spy in Black* (gallant U-Boat Captain Conrad Veidt), *49th Parallel* (the resourceful U-Boat crew), *The Life and Death of Colonel Blimp* (Blimp's Prussian 'oppo', Anton Walbrook), *The Battle of the River Plate* and *Ill Met By Moonlight*.
2   'A Pin to See the Peepshow', *Motion* No 4, 1963 (Ed).

On **The Small Back Room**

The hero of Nigel Balchin's novel is afflicted with alcoholism and a tin leg, ravaged by a case of conscience about a defective gun his boss is pushing, and stalemated by his own imperceptiveness about bureaucratic intrigue; finally he must defuse a German booby-trap bomb. He's also the narrator, and as such gives to understand that he's unhandsome, over the hill, unimpressive of stature and culpably indulgent to moods of self-pity. This narration must reveal to *us* much that the narrator can demonstrate but not state: Sammy's stiff-upper-lip understatements, unemotional statements of emotion (reminiscent of Orwell), his scrupulous team spirit (of his colleagues, it's 'speak no evil'), his excessive self-deprecation (of his heroism he sees only the inadequacy, the mistakes, sees admiration as kindness). We must realise what our narrator does not, e.g. that a senior bureaucrat is sounding him out for promotion, that the colleagues he loyally praises are delinquent, etc. Despite a rather mawkish subtheme about Sammy's be-medalled brother, Balchin expertly achieves a kind of ironic narration (the narrator conveys to the reader crucial information of which he himself is unaware). Such ironies represent a major literary mode and remind us (a) how seriously Brecht underestimated the flexible intricacy of partial alienations within mainstream bourgeois realism; (b) the inadequacy of merely linguistic, literal readings of literary texts; (c) the effectiveness of unstated norms as deconstructions of explicit meanings; and (d) the incompleteness of texts unreferred to a cultural, extra-linguistic, context. The transformation of sign (and sign-cluster, or associative chain) by structure (relationship) is exemplified by Balchin's smooth use of circumstantial detail as thematic counterpointing; e.g. a man in a trilby talking to himself (paralleling the principal narrative as a slightly 'mad' soliloquy), the Train Game (the cynical truths Sammy can't even think of his colleagues are paraphrased, catharted and *lost*, by discussing strangers in trains), the various dream and drunken states in which he sees but doesn't understand the truths his reality-sense skips. The novel ends greyly, Sammy's penultimate heroism may give his soul some private ease, but there's no guarantee that it'll trigger off a tonic aggressivity against bureaucratic creepy-crawlies.

Powell and Pressburger's film works hard to retain most of the book's many plot-strands and sub-issues, but changes the balance between them. David Farrar's dominating physiognomy and presence necessitate a

74

correspondingly more forceful bitterness or neurosis; the film all but recentres on his alcoholism, inspiring the paroxysmatic dream-sequence with a gigantic whisky bottle.[1] The book's feeling against 'the bloody silly way that everything was arranged' is softened, although never quite eclipsed, and a fire-eating one-eyed General (the anti-Blimp) finally presents Rice with his very own research unit. The omission of an intervening NCO puts Sammy in a more heavily paternalistic relationship with an OR's marital troubles. The vignetted Welsh doctor illustrates how P & P can flatten Balchin's extroverted asperities. The book's brief references to xenophobia (are foreigners spies?) are built up (wartime London abounds in ex-allied troops) only to end amiably. Interestingly, P & P ignore most growth points for an *auteurist* version of Balchin's text (e.g. 'Taylor was in his little den with a watchmaker's glass in his eye', 'this colour filter thing').

Remarkably faithful in indicating the book's multiple plot-elements and major themes, the film nonetheless alters its careful equilibrium between the two 'friendly enemies', Sammy and the system, both, in different ways, half-crippled and half-dotty, but ultimately viable. It's poignant that Balchin's Rice's nerves fail just as he must unscrew the boobytrap; and it's this failure that Sammy dwells on (though without self-pity or evasiveness). In the film Rice conquers his nerves, and the bomb, alone. The novel's version permits more intricate, intimate connections between psyche and predicament; and when these inadequacies are (1) incarnated by the powerful Farrar, (2) weakened, and (3) eclipsed by dipsomania with a capital D, the story subtly but pervasively loses its original impetus. The issues tend to interrupt rather than support each other; one is never quite certain what kind of detail to look for as a scene begins; P & P have disobeyed Hitchcock's injunction to 'Clarify! Clarify!', cherishing instead a realistic sophistication (Sue helps Sammy resist drink by offering him one. It's when she isn't there to allow him one that he can't refuse it!). Given the mass audience of the time, a certain disorientation was compounded by P & P's mixture of terse storypointing, an oppressively gloomy atmosphere, and a slightly unorthodox story line. To this conjuntion of factors we attribute the film's mixture of critical success and financial failure.[2]

The novel's first person perspective might have suggested a subjective camera and certain 'impressionistic' effects (given, for example, the behind-the-closing-eyelid viewpoint P & P so splendidly perpetrated in *A Matter of Life and Death*). But given such a topic, an impressionist stress would be irrelevant and distracting, and P & P quite rightly decide that in this case the functional equivalent of any first person impressionism is expressionism. If impressionism centres on perception and expressionism on psychic resonance, both involve mind's-eye-views; and even if, at the extremes at which they are often described, they seem opposite strategies, they can also shade into one another. And while the *story* attenuates Balchin's socially critical stoicism, the film's *style* paraphrases it by

75

atmosphere. What the film loses in crisp narrative impetus, it makes up by a kind of congestion of atmospheres evoking *film noir* at its intensest, i.e. where it shades into expressionism.[3] Thus P & P's film hybridises a stiff upper lip and an expressionist style.[4] The latter does double duty: for Sammy's moods and for blacked-out London.[5] Thus the film brings a *noir* oppressiveness to social reality, without using crime, neurosis or the notion of an underworld as distraction or scapegoat, and belongs to the small and select group of *films noirs* whose flagship is *Citizen Kane*.

Faces moving through alternately opposite spotlights in dark rooms; shadow webs from camouflage netting, window stickytape or elevator grilles; movements now tarry, now knifelike; the sudden cut-ins of a white cat or of abruptly-changed facial expressions; uneasy depths half-obscured by darkness; the then all-but-unique absence of background music, and an off-on noise blitz, achieves an oppressiveness as massive as Lang's; but this is a world of irregularities, of huddles concavities and convexities, of varied angles, of rounded forms. As Campbell Dixon noted, 'Vital conversations take place in offices while automatic drills split the ear and pedestrians pound the grating just above.[6] Almost the only noises we don't hear in this tale of wartime London are those of sirens and guns.' But with the climax we're plunged into an equally relentless decor, the quiet glittering spaces of the beach on which Sammy tackles the unex-ploded bomb, like a little cylinder of concentrated blackness. So sharp a discontinuity runs counter to the craftsman's wisdom of the time; initially, perhaps, dissatisfying, as far as a smooth intensity of mood is concerned, it becomes, on reflection, intriguingly ambiguous. Have the evil shadows retreated into the weapon, into a blessedly definite and obvious enemy of contrast? or do the black and silver worlds finally merge into the film's last poetic realism? is it a deceptive, mocking, and therefore expressionistic, contrast? or do the black and silver worlds finally merge into the film's locale, the dull grey shots of the South Bank (site of the old Shot Tower and the Festival-to-come)? However hesitatingly one advances such an exegesis, one can't put it past authors who earlier contrasted a Technicolor reality with a Socialist utopia in monochrome. There are other deft games with structure: the 'Jerry thermos' with which Stuart tests Sammy's clearheadedness echoes (1) the Highland Whisky which is his inner demon, (2) the final Bomb, and (3) the Shot Tower. The bottle itself becomes a terse paradox. Susan leaves it in Sammy's flat to celebrate V-Day; it's a constant temptation and a constant hope — that one day reality will justify intoxication. The Celtic fringe is still with us: science's painkilling pills din't work, but Highland whisky helps Sammy not to *mind* the pain. The officer who summons Sammy to his test of nerve is named 'Stuart'; the venue, if somewhat displaced (North Wales), is still a part of the wild mountain fringe, of an un-English wildness.[7]

Certain themes and scenes are little masterpieces of quick exposition: the oblique and delicate 'triangle' between Stuart, Sammy and Susan (a plot *non sequitur*), the decisive committee meeting about the dud gun. P &

P remain the only directors to lyricise Kathleen Byron's unique mixture of idealism, propriety and a sharp, wild warmth; she seems to me an icon of the era. The timing of dramatic beats is strange and masterly: close-ups of a white cat *suddenly* introduce a domestic *tempolessness*, while P & P know just how darkness transforms tempo. The DTs sequence introduces a gigantic whisky bottle but, just as we brace ourselves for the climax of the nightmare, the sequence *ejects* us into a different reality (the telephone summons Sammy to confront his 'dark tower'-in-miniature.)

Conceivably P & P (rather than Balchin) had a certain moral in mind. Somehow British 'spirit' has become a little ingrown; it needs an old-fashioned directness, like the General's. Not that things are quite so simplistic. Pinker, the sour-lipped, Machiavellian bureaucrat, is a man of action, while Sammy's friendly colleague (the young Jack Hawkins, smiling oddly like Kenneth More's Bader) is not. From one angle, the film is a third reflection on Britain's powers of self-renewal, alongside *Blimp* and *Matter of Life and Death*. From another angle, it's the first of the more anxious state-of-Britain films, like *The Man in the White Suit* and *Man in the Sky*. It's also one of several touching on relationships between science and wartime loyalty. Ustinov's eupeptic *School for Secrets* and Michael Anderson's *The Dam Busters* both celebrate, in different ways, a slightly surprising harmony of scientists and services. A counterstrain of films (the Boultings' *Seven Days to Noon* and *Suspect*, also based on a Balchin novel, and Dearden-Relph's *The Mind-Benders*) fears scientists' objectivity quickly becoming aloof arrogance and treason.[9] The nexus of feelings, too complex to unravel here, involves not only the utopian and leftist leanings of '30s intellectuals, but residues from another moral elitism, H. G. Wells' 'Open Conspiracy'.[10] The urge to over-'auteurise' P & P could lead one to celebrate the film's virtuosos *strangeness* at the expense of its middle of the road, down to earth qualities, and the massive shot of *realism* in its 'poetic realism'. The little cameos of Pinker intriguing, with his paradoxically exhilarating venom, distills a philosophy into a face with a vivid veracity that out-documentaries any documentary (which is, after all, a major function of fiction). It's all these 'intersections' between private, public and 'poetic' worlds which give this film the restless changing intensity that rewards innumerable viewings, and makes it, in the end, not a 'story one follows', but a sensibility in which one bathes.

1978

1   Certain copies of the film now circulating in England lack it, and at least three other sequences: our first introduction to Professor Mair's research unit, some pub exchanges between Sammy and allied troops, and their return home with him.
2   *The Man in the Grey Flannel Suit*, a few years later, indicates Hollywood's cinematically lumbering, texturally implausible, but more widely and immediately comprehensible, exposition of an in certain ways similar subject.

3 A colleague always miscalls it *The Small Black Room*, which fits.

4 A hybrid less freaky than one might think. Most of Sternberg's heroes keep stiff-upper-lips, and so, in a sense, does Marlene (her fantasticated facial expressions are a kind of tantalising camouflage).

5 It's of the film's essence that we can't be sure where Sammy's mind leaves off and the outside world begins, what's a private darkness and what's a collective one; it corresponds to the misconceptions in the novel's narrative.

6 Not such an irrelevance; in this film all feet, walks and dances recall Sammy's tin leg.

7 Christopher Wicking reads the pills/Scotch juxtaposition in a more complex way. Sammy's mind is prey to barbiturates and alcohol taken alternately and together; in all innocence, he is a drug-abuser; the immensity of the dream bottle is altogether justified.

8 It's tempting to place the telephone, so prominent in this film, in the thermos-bottle-bomb series; it's as impossible to prove as to rule out.

9 There are interesting intersections between *The Small Back Room* and Richard Lester's *Juggernaut*, whose unconvincing story nonetheless gives some leeway to Lester's sharp and saturnine sensibility. The films would make an intriguing double-bill, especially as contrasts in style and content.

10 Balchin is a (non-mandarin) colleague of C. P. Snow's.

3 Watching Death at Work

An Analysis of *A Matter of Life and Death*

John Ellis

> What a vanity is painting which excites our admiration by its resemblance to things, the originals of which do not admire at all.
>
> Picasso quoting Pascal, reported in G Seldes,
> *Movies for the Millions* (1937)

> Highly organised hallucinations comparable to an experience in real life, a combination of vision, hearing and of ideas.
>
> Dr Reeves in *A Matter of Life and Death*

I have several reasons for choosing to analyse this film. I make no apology for subjecting such a pleasurable film to so serious an analysis: first, because it seems to me that any writing which proposes in some way to duplicate the pleasure possible in a film is an enterprise doomed to futility; second, because the particular pleasures gained from this film seem rather disturbing: people want to name them, understand them. This then is the first reason. The film has a strong narrative yet nevertheless succeeds in disturbing the habitual assumptions of narrative films. Further, it seems to begin to criticise the whole equation between cinema and reality that is a central tenet of so much British film-making and criticism alike. Certainly the critics at the time recognised this when the film was selected for the first ever Royal Command Performance. Most of them did not care for the experience very much. This is a second reason: the film has an exemplary place in British cinema, marking the definitive point where the quality critics, engaged in defining a 'native British realism' became disenchanted with the very different work of Powell and Pressburger.

A third reason is more pragmatic. A good 16mm print of the film is in circulation (at least Rank still make it available), a print that is in some ways better than the 35mm nitrate print in the Archive. It has the important feature of having been produced by the original Technicolor method, with a distinctive and brilliant colour quality.*

This analysis is not offered as complete, as reading it will make clear. It falls into four sections: the first describes the film to some extent; the second considers the difficulties that it presented for contemporary film reviewing and criticism; the third tries to explain some of the terms used in the analysis; the fourth is the analysis of the film itself.

1   Descriptions

Two descriptions of *A Matter of Life and Death* follow. One is the plot synopsis released by the publicity machine for the film at the time of its release. The second is a description established from the National Film Archive print, breaking the film down informally into sequences, and emphasising certain moments: those of transition between colour and monochrome, and those of particular interest for the ensuing analysis. The differences between the two reveal a certain amount about how the film was regarded in 1946.

A. THE OFFICIAL PLOT SYNOPSIS

Squadron Leader Peter Carter is returning from his 67th bombing operation. His plane is flying on one engine and a bit, his controls have been shot away, his parachute destroyed and his undercarriage gone. But for the body of his wireless operator he is alone in the plane, and the rest of the crew have baled out. It is beyond belief that he can continue to live after his plane has crashed or he himself has baled out — without a parachute. During what he feels to be the last minute of his life he talks to an American WAC through the wireless transmitter. Because he is a poet and because she is young and lovely and alive, he talks to her of love and poetry — then he jumps. In the Other World the law of order and accuracy has become unbalanced. The French Conductor who has been on duty since the French Revolution has lost his head again and failed to collect Peter Carter at the time he was due to check in. In this world, Peter has met June, the WAC he has already spoken to on the radio. They fall in love but their happiness is threatened by a series of visits which Peter receives from the French Conductor who tries to persuade him to take his rightful place in the Other World. June introduces Peter to an English doctor who lives in a village close to the air station. Although Dr Reeves works as a country practitioner, he has won some recognition in medical circles for his studies of mental diseases. He believes that the visits Peter receives from the Other World are the hallucinations of a sick man whose mind is being affected

---

*   The film was produced in 1946 by the Technicolor three-strip dye transfer process. This mechanically based, labour intensive process is now being phased out by Technicolor, its use recently has been limited to the manufacture of high quality release prints for certain discerning producers and directors. Soon, it will be available only in the People's Republic of China, where Technicolor have just sold a dye-transfer plant. In the 1950's the process was supplanted for shooting (and, increasingly, release print) purposes by cheaper colour-sensitive chemical stocks. The advantages of the dye-transfer process are that it gives the possibility of more subtle colour manipulation in print production, a generally higher colour saturation, and has none of the problems of deterioration to which chemically-based colour stocks are prone as they age.

almost to the point of death. But Peter wants to live. His love for June gives him the strength to parry the diplomat who tries so constantly to win him over to the Other World. Finally, his visitor tells him that he is to be allowed to appeal in the High Court. He is to appeal on the grounds that, through the inefficiency of the Conductor, he was allowed 'borrowed' time in this world during which he found himself with a new earthly responsibility — he fell in love.

As Counsel for Defence in the Other World, Peter has the choice of the great minds of all nations, from Plato to Pitt, from Caesar to Richelieu. But he cannot believe that any of them could ably defend him on the simple evidence of being in love. Also he knows that the Prosecuting Counsel is an American with a strict anti-English bias — Abraham Farlan, the first American to die of an English bullet during the War of Independence. Meanwhile, Dr Reeves' research proves that complications arising from a slight concussion are affecting Peter's brain and only a highly skilled operation can save him. A weakening in Peter's condition as the time for his Trial draws nearer, causes the doctor to set off for an ambulance during a heavy storm. As he rushed through the night on his motorcycle he collides with the ambulance and is killed.

Arriving in the Other World, the doctor is told that Peter has chosen him as his Counsel for the Defence. So while the finest surgeons available are fighting to save Peter's life in this world, the doctor is fighting for him in the Other. The huge amphitheatre of the High Court is filled with every nationality of every historical age. With their ancestors who fought great wars against us, sit the soldiers, sailors and airmen who fought with us. Among them are Americans, including Abraham Farlan who brings as evidence against an Englishman, who wishes to marry an American girl, his English heritage. A heritage which an American of the War of Independence scorns. Farlan introduces the jury to the doctor — a jury composed of Russian, French, Chinese, Dutch, Irish — and challenges the doctor to find any member of it that has not cause for prejudice against England. He swears that any jury the doctor chooses to call will bear the same prejudice. America is the only country in which individual rights are inalienable. Doctor Reeves calls for an American jury. They file in one by one but are still seen to be composed of mixed nationalities — but they are all American citizens. Further, Dr Reeves discovers that Farlan's own grandfather was an Englishman.

With historical prejudice swept away it only remains to prove that Peter and June are truly in love. The High Court visits the theatre in which the operation is being performed on Peter, and where June is sleeping exhaustedly. While the surgeon is still at work Peter moves away from his body to be questioned by Farlan. Farlan grants that he is in love. Now June is called upon to prove her love.

Her love for Peter is so strong that she agrees to take his place in the Other world. In spite of Peter's protests, she steps on the great escalator that is to take her there. She moves higher and higher, further away from Peter. The doctor watches anxiously. But suddenly the escalator stops — the mechanism is not strong enough to tear the two lovers from each other. Although in the Universe nothing is stronger than Law, in this world nothing is stronger than love.

In a private ward of the hospital, Peter returns to consciousness. The operation has been successful. He has won his case. He lives.

B. BRIEF SEQUENCE ANALYSIS (BASED ON NFA 35mm NITRATE PRINT)

Length in ft.		Reel 1
0	Seq 1	BBFC 'A' Cert/b&w *Rank Organisation Presents*/The Archers' trademark (target) b&w fading to colour as arrow hits target/Titles (white on plain blue): *David Niven/Roger Livesey/Raymond Massey/A Matter of Life and Death/Kim Hunter/Marius Goring/Written, Produced and Directed by Michael Powell and Emeric Pressburger.*
191		Rolling caption: *This is the story of two worlds, the one we know and another which exists only in the mind of a young airman whose life and imagination have been violently shaped by war.*/(in italics) *Any resemb-*

		lance to any other world, known or unknown, is purely coincidental.
230	2	Panning shot across the universe, voice-over pointing out significant features: stars, gas, an exploding solar system, a globular cluster, etc. *'Nearer home'* — the moon, earth — *'part of the universe, reassuring isn't it?'* v/o becomes urgent to describe night over Europe after a bombing raid. A burning German city, fog, noises mixed below which become dominant (radio, foghorns, etc; one message comes out of the cacophony, followed by sudden cut to
350	3	Brief shot of plane with one wing in flames; pan across wrecked to Bob's corpse and Peter shouting into radio. Conversation follows, intercutting Peter with June in control tower, both in MS and CU variously.
990		Peter jumps without parachute, camera follows through hatch until screen is filled with grey fog; sound: rushing wind and, increasingly confused, Peter's last words to Bob, *'prop or wings'*, repeated over and over. Cut
1106	4	Cut to sea breaking gently on shore, seen from plane, fade to rows of angelic wings in b&w Bob waiting for Peter at aircrew check-in for the other world; **several airmen arrive, including a group of Americans; Bob increasingly worried, but assured mistakes are virtually impossible.**

Reel 2

0		Bob reluctantly signs entry register. Ticking of clock fades to similar music as image cuts to
85	5	Seashore at dawn. Peter awakes, casts off excess clothing, meets dog and naked shepherd boy playing flute; realises he is still on earth. Sees girl on bike and pursues; meets June; her recognition of him as the pilot, cut to
523	6	CU of the other world's register, with deficit of one, colour fades to b&w. A female administrator is sorting out the muddle after Peter's 19 hr 50 min absence. Conductor 71 (Marius Goring, a French aristocrat executed in 1791) lost him in the fog; now sent to bring him back by explaining the situation; Bob sends a message — dolly into rose on 71's lapel: it 'becomes' coloured pink by dissolves.
760	7	Dolly out to 71 amongst rhododendrons. He finds Peter and June, and 'stops time' as Peter offers her a drink — he is still conscious, she is not. Conversation between Peter and 71: Peter appeals to reason, on which laws are based, refuses to come. 71 admires June, but defeated, fades out: halfway through the fade, returns with an afterthought about chess, then disappears.
1350		**June refuses drink. Peter disorientated; June's doubt about what he tells her; Peter headache.**
1530		Subjective shot from Peter's POV — June obscured by haze towards left
1550		of screen. Peter: *'I thought I'd lost you'*, as he holds her.

Reel 3

0	8	Phone at Dr Reeves' answered by cleaner, who tells caller (June) that he is in his *'thing, you know, camera obscura'*. Cut to bored dogs listening to
25		Reeves' (Roger Livesey) remarks about the village. General shot of Reeves operating camera obscura and 'panning' image of village street shot through camera obscura showing lens, gearing and table beneath, cut to image filling screen: June arriving. Doctor opens shutters, dolly over table to frame door; June comes up, operates camera obscura (general shot as before); conversation about Peter. Reeves has already arranged to take up the case; casts humorous doubt on reality of June's love for Peter. *'I'll be over about tea-time.'*
367	9	Dissolve to chickens scattered by motorcycle; Reeves races with Americans in jeep and wins by risky cornering.
454	10	Dissolve sound then image to Mendelssohn's *Midsummer Night's Dream* over scenes of activity preparing for a performance at the US airbase. A

poster, portrait; vicar rehearsing American cast. Bottom: *'Some man or other must present Wall; and let him have some plaster, or some loam, or some rough-cast about him, to signify wall; and let him hold his fingers thus, and through that cranny shall Pyramus and Thisbe whisper.*(III, i, 72-6), with business that allows private to hit his officer; CU/ record ending; CU/hands on piano, ominous minor-key music; Peter looking distracted from chess game with June (first general shot of hall, all previous actitivies in scene found to be dispersed in this same space), ambient sounds mixed down until June disturbs his reverie. Reeves appears, mentions Peter's poetry,

670   which he admires, questions Peter about his life and his hallucinations. Tests his visual perception: stands behind Peter, tells him to concentrate on a girl (cut to general shot from Peter's POV: girl in centre frame), then describe what is to extreme right and left. As he does so, shot held of Peter and Reeves, after Peter describes curtains to the extreme left, cut to general shot shifted to left: banks of roses clearly visible in front of curtains), June's remark, *'When you two have quite finished looking at that girl's legs';* cut to MCU/ Peter answering, then checking his guess about the curtains and looking disconcerted. Conversation continues, exchange about death and survival of the human personality; Reeves complains about lateness of tea; will take Peter to his house; tea arrives, Vicar: *'We're shaping'.* Fade out to black.

11   Fade to Peter asleep amongst books, 90° dolly reveals source of sounds of table-tennis: Reeves and June playing on the covered veranda outside the window, Reeves at far end of table. Reverse angle framing Reeves; shot framing Reeves and one side of table from open side of veranda, pans

1195   rapidly following his service to June, and continues to pan from side to side following the ball five more times. June asks about Peter's drugged state, challenges Reeves' knowledge of Peter. She lets the game end, they go into the study, stand in front of Peter discussing his state, Reeves: *'He is having highly organised hallucinations comparable to an experience in real life, a combination of vision, hearing and of idea'.* They conspire to invent a lie about how he survived if his state worsens, and return to the game, this time a long shot framing both players from the open side of the veranda,

1490   with one more play than the last service. Another service and the image is frozen with the ball in mid-flight; Peter awakes, sees 71, rings bell to warn

1588   the others, but it is silent, runs, knocking over a pile of books without sound; shouts but finds June and Reeves frozen.

       Reel 4

0   71 picks up a book on chess, replaces the table (reverse motion); conversation in two-shot reframing as 71 moves to and fro: 71 displays his powers, *'What is time? . . . a mere tyranny'.* Peter allowed to appeal but Abraham Farlan is prosecuting counsel; 71 disappears behind Peter; cut to table tennis game resumed (2 fast pans), then bell heard. Reeves and June rush in, Peter reports his meeting, Reeves tests his reflexes; June asks to stay, Peter wants to sleep in study; housekeeper busies herself with the arrangements. Peter worried about chess book that 71 has borrowed, and about who to choose to defend him; Reeves: *'Here on earth I'm your*

495   *defending counsel'.*

12   Dissolve to Army Hospital sign, dolly follows Reeves to washroom to consult with Dr McEwan; insists operation must be that night because of Peter's trial, explains the hallucinations: *'incredibly detailed . . . nothing is entirely fantastic. It is invention, but logical invention'.* Pan to white wall with

740   shadow of venetian blinds.

13   Dissolve to b&w vast escalator with Peter and 71 sitting on steps as it.

1020		ascends, trying to select his defence counsel from the statues of famous men arrayed along the way. Peter decides on 'an ordinary Englishman', realises the escalator is carrying him to the Other World, runs back down; 71's 'Peter come back' fades into June's voice as CU of Peter distraught dissolves to colour.
	14	The ambulance is late; the phone is dead; Reeves goes on his motorbike to fetch it.
1380	15	He meets the ambulance on a bend, swerves to avoid it and is killed by the explosion of the fuel tank.
1398	16	CU Peter in ambulance.

Reel 5

0		Conversation in ambulance: Peter asks about Reeves. June eventually tells. Peter turns his head away. Peter is taken out of the ambulance. Peter's
170		POV shot of corridor roof in hospital; CU Peter, eyes open; Peter's POV of June, more roof, nurses discussing his case, greeting him, fade to CU Peter's head bandaged. Peter's POV of light for operation; long shot whole operating theatre with June looking through glass doors; CU June; medium shot Peter and nurses surrounding him, dolly/pan in so that camera takes up Peter's POV as mask is lowered over his face; CU Peter looking; shot from within Peter's eye as it closes, pan down/dissolve to swirling lights and patterns becoming progressively more blue until dissolve to
320	17	stadium in Other World, crowds entering in very long shot. 71 is waiting for Reeves who arrives with his conductor, John Bunyan. Reeves is to defend Peter, and asks to see his client, taking Bob as witness; Bob dissolves into colour whilst background figures remain monochrome; cut to
511	18	operating Theatre, characters frozen; Peter pops up from under sheets, walks through glass door with 71 to where June is standing. They cluster around her, discussing the case and their lack of evidence; Peter asks to kiss her, even though she won't feel anything; a tear appears on her cheek;
746*		71 catches it on a rose to take it with them; CU rose it fades to monochrome ...
810	19	pull out from rose as it is put onto perspex table; establishing shots of court arena, and of audience, grouped according to occupation: US airmen; WAAF's; nurses; Bob and the admissions clerk among these groups; Sikh soldiers; A British regiment from the American War of Independence;
1079*		French Revolutionaries; British gentlemen of the 18th century; Quakers. All stand (each group in turn) as Bob turns to speak to the admissions clerk. The judge gives a preamble. Farlan opens the case for the prosecution, a long argument follows, concentrating on Farlan and Reeves, with intercut reactions to certain remarks by various groups. Farlan's argument stresses the nationalities of Peter and June, calling wartime romance the passion of the moment, saying USA came to the aid of Britain, not to become its prisoners: 'We are all as God made us, but our grandparents had a deal to do in the shaping of us.' Reeves agrees; Farlan's grandfather left Britain because he didn't like it, and he would like it even less now: evidence, a radio
1600		broadcast of a cricket match, the voice of England 1945. 71 disappears from behind Reeves.

Reel 6

0		71 reappears with a radio which plays the voice of America 1945: jazz.

---

* 50 feet concerning the tear appear with French subtitles in the Archive print. (746-801). This reel also has a few short pieces missing towards the end.

Farlan disconcerted. Reeves says he does not understand it either. Reeves calls great English poets as his witnesses, saying Peter will be one of them, given time. Fade to

104   **20**   oxygen valve for operation, surgeon drilling, June waiting, breathing suddenly accelerates, concern, it subsides. Cut to

180   **21**   Farlan's summary: a diatribe against England for its discomfort, slowness etc. To Reeves' challenge that Peter, not Britain, is on trial, he repeats that character is formed by a chain of circumstance, quoting Ben Franklin. Reeves counters with a quote from Washington on the supreme value of conscience (Washington being born English), and accuses Farlan of trying to prejudice the jury. Farlan claims that a jury drawn from any nation would be anti-British, and demonstrates; a Frenchman (wars every century); a Boer; a Russian (the Crimean war); a Chinese (the 1837 occupation of an unprotected Peking); a Punjabi ('think of India, Dr Reeves', cut-in of group of Sikh soldiers); an Irishman. Reeves wants to change the jury. Farlan agrees with the proviso it should not include English people. A discussion on respect for the rights of the individual follows, Reeves emphasising the practical liberties of the English, Farlan giving a rousing speech about the high ideals of the Americans. Reeves rises to the challenge and requests a jury of Americans, as they will defend the rights of the individual against the law. Farlan emphasises that nothing in the Universe is stronger than the Law, Reeves counterposes this with Justice. The jury is changed by a series of dissolves to American citizens with foreign names and accents: a chef (French); a soldier (Dutch); a cab driver (Russian); a smart young man holding a MOMA catalogue (Chinese); a soldier (black); a cop (Irish). Reeves pleads true love, offering the tear as evidence. The jury asks to see the defendant for themselves; camera pulls out from the stadium until it becomes the Milky Way; a shaft of light appears, the escalator with the jury, judge etc. on it. Cut to

     22   operating theatre with escalator behind the frozen group of surgeons and nurses. Peter appears in RAF flying gear, Farlan questions about the reality of his love. June is brought as a witness; she offers to go to the Other World instead of Peter; he refuses to let her, proving his love to Farlan; Reeves says it is the only way to prove the strength of their love, Farlan warns that nothing is stronger than the Law. June mounts the escalator which begins to move; suddenly stops, showing that, although nothing is stronger than the Law in the universe, there is nothing stronger than love on earth. The judge sums up with 'as Sir Walter Scott is always saying', several lines ending 'Love is Heaven and Heaven is Love'. The verdict is for the defendant, and Peter is given a new date of arrival in the other world, 'the rights of the uncommon man must always be respected'. Fade to

     23   operating theatre. The surgeon takes off his mask: it is the Judge. Peter with a dressing on his head. 71 on the escalator which is fading away throws the 'lost' chess book back; the book spirals down over a wipe that progressively reveals a holdall being unzipped: June finds the book in Peter's jacket pocket; Peter asks for Reeves in his sleep, awakes as the nurse opens the curtains and says to June 'We won, darling.' 'Yes I know'.

1650   **24**   End titles

2   *Press Reception*

Quoting contemporary reviews is often a futile process: they are taken as 'evidence' for what concrete audience reaction(s) would have been to the film. This ignores the nature of the institution of journalism, and the function of film reviewing within the industry. What reviews can reveal is a certain relationship: that between a film, and a privileged group who operate with remarkably similar aesthetic presumptions. In this case, the reviews of *A Matter of Life and Death* indicate that it is in tension with the critics' prevaililng assumptions, even though they grudgingly admit having gained a certain amount of pleasures. It even incites two or three prestige critics into a definition of their preferred aesthetic: realism.

The terms of praise of the film are virtually all in the form of a 'yes, but . . .'. The warmest defender marks a double distance (from Powell and Pressburger, from the 'anti-British' slant): 'Other people have thought more highly of some of the Powell-Pressburger films than I. It is with all the more pleasure that I recommend *A Matter* as one of the most original stimulating and entertaining films ever made in England . . . This is by no means to say that I think the film faultless'. (*Daily Telegraph*, 1.11.46). Others are more measured: 'In a way, indeed, this a technician's film, depending for many of its effects on the trick shot . . . Visual narrative, cinematic sense: there is no denying the quality of the film in excitement, tension, pictorial shock. The quality of its imagination is another matter.' (Dilys Powell, *Sunday Times*, 3.11.46); 'charm and extreme technical efficiency' (*Motion Picture Herald*, 16.11.46); 'a remarkable film the story of which does not bear too rigorous an examination, though it is undoubtedly an imaginative technical feat of great interest'. (Roger Manvell, *BFI 'Records of the Film'* series). Praise for the technical, for cinematic sense, but always reservations.

Reservations express themselves across several ideas: the value or sensitivity of its central premises; the way in which attention wandered; inability to decide how the film was 'intended'. 'From the beginning the situation is melodramatic rather than dramatic or poetic; the characters . . . are the characters of journalism and the novelette. And the central problem emerges as trivial . . . The lovers here are cinema lovers, without depth as they are without virtue or sin; they meet, speak, vow by the rules of celluloid'. (Dilys Powell). 'Complete absence of one factor vital to the cinema: the dramatic link with real-life people and their problems'. (*Tribune*). 'It misses importance because it is not consistent, and exploits rather than examines its central theme and chief characters. It has vitality, ingenuity and wit, but not, unfortunately, a poet's feeling for the implications of the story' (Roger Manvell). 'It would seem, too, that the main point of the film is not that it has anything new or important or even comprehensible to tell us about life and death and psychology but that, with such a theme, there are abundant opportunities for cinematic tricks. It is as though Hitchcock's *Spellbound* were combined with all those familiar films about invisible men.' (*Times*). 'Was it then the main purpose of the film to preach international friendship? If so, the purpose was most worthy but the effect was pure bathos.' (*Times*). So, the first terms of criticism: disappointment in the psychology of the characters, uncertainty about its meaning.

The *Times* critic identifies this uncertainty with the abundance of technical 'tricks'. This theme is extended by other critics: 'leaves us in grave doubt whether it is intended to be serious or gay'. (C. A. Lejeune, *Observer*, 3.11.46); 'a grandiose anarchy' (*Times*); 'This could have been great if the directors believed in it. The trouble is they don't. Or not with their whole hearts. The result is less passion than whimsy' (*Sunday Graphic*, 3.11.46). Critics are uncertain about how they are being addressed by the film, whether they are 'meant' to take it as this kind of film or that, whether there is a fundamental belief expressed in the film's content. This uncertainty in the face of the film is taken further in two ways; either by condemning the film's inconsistency and bad taste, or by talking about wandering attention. Condemnation; 'One has met this kind of embarrassment before with Messrs Powell and Pressburger, so fluent and prodigal of style, so moodily inept in story. When will they tune their fantasy to their material? Everything is at odds, except the purely cinematic skill, in this latest gamble with worlds.' (*Time and Tide*, 9.11.46). Bad taste: 'Also on the debit side are the deplorably inapposite gags dragged in for a cheap laugh, referring to a Technicolor-less Other World and a recent British film. In a film of this importance, such sallies are in the worst possible taste and totally indefensible.' (*Today's Cinema*, 5.11.46). Wandering attention: 'The novel cosmic introduction and the initial shots of the hero's blazing bomber give the film an impressive start, but for the next 20 minutes or so it is somewhat difficult to get the gist of the joke, if any. Doubts are, however, rapidly dispelled immediately that it is clear that the fabulous 'not of this world' sequences are devised to illustrate the hero's hallucinations.' (*Kine Weekly*, 7.11.46). 'There were about 40 minutes in the first half of the film when I just couldn't decide whether it was a great achievement or not. It had given me a laugh or two, and made me goggle over some of the photography and effects. But I hadn't been moved. Here was a fine theme being seriously treated. Yet no crawling around the back of my hair, nothing to tense me or make me catch my breath. And then came a scene [where June's tear is caught on the rose (seq. 18)] — well, there was a sort of click inside me and I said to my wife: "Well, they've done it". (*Daily Express*, 2.11.46). All of these criticisms have one thing in common: they resent to some degree or other being held separate from the immediate emotional involvement that they expect from a narrative fiction film. In a serious film, of course, this acquires a moral force, and it is this moral force that is given the name 'realism.'

Two critics are driven by their dissatisfaction with the experience of the film to define their critical criteria: 'even further away from the essential realism and the true business of the British movie than their two recent films *I Know Where I'm Going* and *A Canterbury Tale*' (Richard Winnington, *News Chronicle*, 2.11.46); 'Asquith, Carol Reed, Launder & Gilliatt, the Boultings, Thorold Dickinson and David Lean among others, are establishing a tradition of solid native skill to which the latest production of this better-known combination contributes almost nothing'. (Humphrey

Swingler, *Our Time*, Dec 1946). Both critics refer implicitly to a tradition of realism being developed in Britain. It is this developing tradition from which Powell and Pressburger are in the process of being excluded: they do not conform to its aesthetic *. American criticism, if the available documents are anything to judge by, did not (yet) perceive this as being the case: 'To be recommended to any audience on its orthodox ingredients of appeal. But it's one of these films in which Britain lately has specialised which will attract the discriminating who never normally frequent the motion picture.' (*Motion Picture Herald*, 16.11.46).

What, then, is the nature of this aesthetic, and how does *A Matter of Life and Death* go against it, creating this sense of unease and disappointment? The answer can only be found in a detailed analysis of the film using certain defined theoretical presuppositions.

3 Narrative and Realism

A short note is needed to clarify the analysis of *A Matter* that follows. Two terms in particular need to be explained, narrative and realism. Their interrelationship is the basis of a particularly tenacious ideological operation which *A Matter* seems to try to refuse.

A narrative has a beginning, middle and end: that much everyone knows. But the nature of this process is rather more tricky to define. The beginning of a narrative is more or less the moment of violation of a pre-existent harmony, a moment of dislocation, of troubling, of violence. The end of a narrative then becomes the moment at which this troubling or dislocation is overcome: a new balance and harmony is achieved. So narrative is a process ('the middle') by which first, a state of stasis, harmony, homogeneity is proposed; then, almost immediately, it is shattered: a new element is introduced ('the stranger comes to town'), an outburst of violence shatters the calm, an action that is inexplicable takes place. The various elements of character, place, action are put into turmoil; a troubling spreads from the initial dislocation to affect all the elements contained in the narrative's space. From an initial homogeneity, heterogeneity is produced. The narrative then works to restore a state of homogeneity, to reintegrate all the troubled elements into a new order.

This process of reintegration involves the redefinition of some elements, such as the migration of characteristics from one character to another. It takes place across a series of more or less sequential events, one leading on to another and another, across time. What these events represent is different states of arrangement between the elements, all of them to some extent unsatisfactory: e.g. antagonism between characters becomes enforced co-operation; then uneasy agreement; a testing of the uneasy agreement; and finally a fresh understanding. Such is a typical narrative progression from dislocation, through a string of events, to a final reintegration. This ordered flow of events ensures that the heterogeneity is always

* For a further examination of the aesthetic of such critics, see my 'Art, Culture and Quality: Terms for a Cinema in the Forties and Seventies', *Screen* v. 19 no 3 (Autumn 1978).

controlled, that the potential chaos is always kept within certain bounds. Thus, it is not possible (except by 'losing the thread') to concentrate on meanings that are designated as 'background' to the exclusion of the ostensible subjects of the narration. There is a certain hierarchy maintained within the heterogeneous 'middle' of a narrative that enables the narration of the trouble and its reintegration to take place at all. The trouble is not absolute, a pandemonium, but contained and relative.

There are numerous ways in which this containment is achieved, through the production of a rhythm across the narration, tying it together. The first of these is to produce a balance between meanings that are new to the audience and those which are familiar from the narration already. Too much of one or the other produces a certain sense of anxiety (which is often deliberately exploited). Hence devices of continuity, and the cueing of certain elements which only later reach their full realisation. An example in this film is the play between seq. 9 (reel 3) and seq. 15 (reel 4). There is no real need to show Reeves' journey to have tea with June and Peter at the airbase . . . except that it introduces Reeves' reckless motorcycle driving which in the second sequence, causes his death. The element of Reeves' bike is introduced in a prepared context (we know where he's travelling) so that it is already known when it is produced as a crucial event in the narration. Having fulfilled its function, it is exhausted, used up. This exhaustion of elements is also typical of the way in which a narration is a controlled balance of the new and the familiar: elements perform a useful function and then do not reappear. They are familiar, but do not presume upon their familiarity to the extent of preventing further innovation, further progress of the narration. The fundamental familiar elements across the narrative are not actions, locations, or even usually objects, but characters and the terms of the problem, the dislocation, in which the narrative has involved them. The same bodies move across the screen, accruing to themselves consistent as well as altering characteristics. A controlled play of novelty and familiarity takes place around these recognisable centres.

Another form of the containment of heterogeneity is the production of patterns of similarity and difference across the narration, by the use of such techniques as rhyming and doubling. Rhyming refers to the way in which certain forms of shot (often spectacular; crane shots etc.) are repeated at various points in the text, providing an effect of repetition, of similarity. This can equally be by the use of certain elements of decor, like the roses in *A Matter*, which recurr across the film, providing a moment of purely figurative coherence. Doubling indicates the way in which some characteristics are marked, whereas others stay in the background. At its simplest, this means that a facial expression will become a signification 'to be noticed' only if it is in close-up, or lit to make it stand out from the other possible significations (setting, bodily movement, costume etc.). Very quickly, the means of doubling becomes a part of the rhythm of the narration because of this: its emphases do not remain haphazard and dependent on the immediate context alone, they are systematised, rhythmic.

It is important to emphasise that these processes of containment of the heterogeneous are never, at any point, within the progress of the narration, complete and balanced. There is always a sense of something lacking and something more that hovers over the narration, pushing it on. The patterns that work across the narration are always, during their working, incomplete and in a state of flux; rhymes hang in the air presupposing their mutual echoing without, for a moment, it actually existing; elements disappear, leaving behind a memory that disturbs any possible coherence until they reappear. All this means that although coherence and stasis are the aim of the process of narration, it is an aim that exists across an instability: there is a play between the containment that exists at any time within the narration, and the surplus that will inevitably disturb it.

This play between the heterogeneous, the chaotic, and its always-provisional reintegration, is intelligible only from a certain position. The film is not just coloured lights playing across a screen, nor is it a succession of shots that seem to behave as discreet units with no discernible connection between them. The organisation of a narrative film constructs a certain position of intelligibility for itself. It constructs a position for a subject that it addresses. This position emphasises coherence at the expense of the excess, of the heterogeneous, of the unconscious. The subject of the narration is a unified subject, that of a unified 'I', a position of knowledge and intelligibility for the narration. The heterogeneity of the subject (the network of associations that can be generated from any moment of any film, its light and sounds, its chance concatenations of elements) is contained; process and movement are given pattern and direction for the unification of a subject, the point of the organisation of the narration.

This subject position, the product of the operations of the text, should not be confused with the particular attitude of the spectator towards the realist text: an attitude of separation and involvement, a form of voyeurism. Although the two depend upon each other for their very existence, there is a crucial difference. The positioning of the subject is a question of the installation of a kind of rationality where such does not necessarily exist: the idea of subject position is concerned to emphasise the construction of a division conscious/unconscious, of a form of ordering and hierachisation within the heterogeneous, in order to produce an intelligibility. The spectator's attitude finds its basis within this subject positioning, but it is rather an attitude towards the narration, towards cinematic narrative as a whole. It rests upon the play of subject position, always slightly different depending upon the containments operating within the narration, but is a rational attitude, the attitude of an already-constituted 'I'. The difference can be summed up: the subject is felt by the narration, the spectator feels.

The spectator, thinking and rational, is able to choose, to judge, to form opinions about the narration. The spectator is able to do this on the basis of the subject position, the position of intelligibility, produced by the film across its narration. Subject position is an effect of the narration, the spectator's attitude is built upon this effect. The spectator is therefore in a position of separation and involvement at once: outside the narration ('where it makes sense'), and within the narrative (concerned for the characters and situation, taking the film as a playing-through of phantasies in a displaced way). The spectator's attitude involves a kind of voyeurism: watching, without being watched, characters who have agreed not to acknowledge that they are being watched. On the basis of the construction by the film of a coherent 'I' to which it is addressed, the spectator can become the 'eye' that is the final gaze (apart from that of a god) in the play of gazes (spectator-screen, camera-event, character-character).

It has to be said that this is broad generalisation about narrative. The effects of subject position and spectator attitude are not the same for all narratives: the particular forms of narrative process (the particular discursive form, or 'genre') place the subject in a slightly different relation of coherence, involving a different relation of containment, a different ordering of the heterogeneous. *A Matter of Life and Death* begins to disrupt the process of subject positioning by providing more than one point of intelligibility, by providing two regimes of coherence for the subject: that of a narrative love-story, and that of a more 'documentary' mode of exposition and explanation. This is one central aspect to the film: in providing differing and therefore conflicting modes of address, it begins to disrupt some features of the subject position of both modes.

The particular form of disruption that *A Matter of Life and Death* offers is one that questions the nature of cinematic realism. Realism in the cinema is an effect, an effect produced both by the construction by the text of a unitary subject position for its intelligibility across the processes of narration, and equally by the assumption by the spectator of an attitude of knowledge, of unproblematic observation upon this basis. The effect of this unitary subject position and unproblematic form of viewing, typical of almost all narrative film at the moment of its initial manufacture within the cinematic apparatus at least, is that the film presents to the spectator an effect of reality. It seems as though reality speaks rather than a particular highly developed system of signification with its attendant patterning of the heterogeneous. The spectator is unaware of the position into which he/she is put. It seems as though a dialogue takes place: reality speaks, the spectator attends; reality displays itself, the spectator admires. A whole process has effaced itself modestly behind this satisfying claim. The 'mechanics' of the enunciation of dislocations between elements (themselves the products of signification) across the construction of patterns of containment — all these rather arcane processes smooth themselves over by their very effectivity in placing the subject as a particular position of knowledge and coherence that the said spectator is only too willing to take up. The spectator sees reality; subject positioning remains unseen.

Reality speaks, an effect of realism is achieved. But it is not the same effect of reality that is achieved in three films whose release coincided with that of *A Matter of Life and Death*, three films which demonstrate the effectivity at this time of the ideological operation that is known as realism (it is assuredly an effect of ideology to deny the troubling force of the unconscious by confirming the coherence of an 'I', and at the same time to present not discourse and signification but reality itself for the inspection of the eye of a spectator). The films in question are *The Best Years of Our Lives*, *My Darling Clementine* and *The Beast With Five Fingers*, (all released around Christmas 1946), all in their way exemplary films in achieving different effects of reality through narrative.

The realism of *The Best Years of Our Lives*, a fresh new quality, is described by contemporary critics in terms of morality and photography. It is moral in the sense that the subject is provided with a perfect position of unseen mastery, seeing clearly groups of people as they interact, unaware that they are watched. This position is never perceived as such, instead it enables the serious business of sympathy with characters and their complicated situations to flourish. Its morality is then founded upon the very effectivity of its subject-positioning, and the assumption by the spectator of a voyeurism with no awareness that a position is being taken up at all. This realism is photographic because it produces, through deep focus photography, the startling effect of 'not being a photograph'. The range of the visible is extended remarkably, enabling the spectator to have the impression of looking around within the frame rather than being directed to look at a particular fragment of an event. The effect of reality gained from this was considerable, as the image seems to go beyond anything that had been achieved in the conventional photographic image. It was as though photography and montage disappeared. This disappearance of the technical intensified the effect of reality produced by subject-positioning in relation to the narration.

My Darling Clementine operates within the norms which *The Best Years* exceeds. What it provides is a more classic narrative, that is, a system of balance between repetition and novelty within the narration that is balanced according to current conventions. Again, it provides a security for the spectator; and, rather than a 'moral' realism, it demonstrates a supreme confidence in the means of the realist narrative: one single shot is enough to provide all the terms of the conflict: Earps driving their cattle across the prairie, Clantons in their buckboard, watching in the foreground. It is this confidence in the institution of classic narrative cinema that can provide the basis for an illusionist horror film cycle of which Warners' *The Beast with Five Fingers* is a late representative. A disembodied hand haunts a timid secretary: the supernatural here depends on the natural, on the achievement of a classic narrative form that will produce virtually the same position for the subject as that of *Clementine*.

These three films represent the strength of the realist narrative in 1946. Nowadays such confidence no longer exists, at least in the cinema, and the effect of reality is increasingly something that needs to be worked over afresh with each production. However, for a film of 1946 to undermine the conditions for the easy production of this effect was something that critics found disconcerting when they noticed it at all. As we have seen, the quality critics, partisans of the nascent British realism, expressed their profound reservations about *A Matter*. This was only to be expected, since, as we can now see, the film expresses a series of profound reservations about the realist aesthetic and realist filmmaking.

4 A Matter of Life and Death

The film poses an order very strongly at the outset, after the titles. The sequence (seq. 2) is disconcerting to say the least: it gives a colour documentary-style tour of the universe. The exposition of the universe demonstrates cataclysmic events that nevertheless have a place in a reassuring order to which we are the unmoved spectators (a cosmic explosion is explained by the comforting male voice-over: 'There goes another solar system; someone's been mucking about the uranium atom again. Don't worry, it's not ours'.). The mode of address is that of documentary, an exposition of facts for the intellectually curious given from a point of easy authority. It conveys (never states) the conception of an order to the universe which places even the most cataclysmic events, an order which finds its equivalent in the descriptive physics of the commentary. It is disconcerting enough as the beginning of a fiction film; the troubling of the coherence of classic narrative that it represents becomes a constituent part of the film's system.

As the leisurely pan across the stars rests on our moon and finally the earth itself, the commentary becomes more urgent, finally inviting us to listen to the voices in the night air. The transition from documentary exposition to fictional narrative is effected: the voice gains an emotional intensity (suddenly), and absents itself having invited the spectator to listen to sounds that belong to the fictional space, the diegesis of the fiction. A disruption of the easy homogeneity of the universe is beginning: it still has to be specified, however. The initial specifications are produced in sequence 3. Two central characters are introduced, 'the man and the girl' as Powell engagingly put it, 'old hat, but played this way, terribly exciting.' (Gough-Yates, 1971, p10). The emotional pull of the sequence is its impossibility: a doomed airman shouting out his last messages (poetry, telegram to mother, questions about the girl he's speaking to), and June bravely responding, though her voice falters and tears well up in her eyes. It is an intolerable event, precisely because it is so much within conventions (of the brave last message; of the first encounter between characters clearly destined to become lovers), and at the same time frustrating those conventions (the last message refuses to accept death, affirming the exuberance of living; the love between them is doomed because of Peter's inevitable death, because they have never even seen each other). The pathos of the sequence is produced by the wild mixture of conventions which themselves are to some extent frustrated, refused their 'habitual' outcomes, and equally by the dislocation that works between them ('last message' v. 'beginning of love story').

Through the constant cutting to June's reaction shots, the patterning typical of a love story gradually gains strength through the sequence: what is being effected through the interchanges between the two characters is the initiation of a love-story, an attraction is posed both explicitly ('I like the sound of your voice'; 'I wish I could have met you') and implicitly (through the cutting between the characters *as though* this were a shot/reverse shot set-up: Peter in medium close-up looking off-screen right, and June in medium close-up looking off-screen left). It is a love-story that seems impossible. There is no doubt about the outcome of the story, there is no doubt about how it could proceed, in short there seems no possibility of a narrative. Peter will die, June and he will never have met. For the love-story itself, there is no problem to be resolved: it is pointless, predetermined.

Yet this frustrated love-story comes itself as a disruption, a disruption of the harmony of the universe, where all events make sense, and no events involve the spectator. There is, in other words, a radical disjunction of address generated between sequences 2 and 3. The documentary form of seq. 2 is expository, placing the spectator as separate from events which can be placed, comprehended, mastered. The initiation of the narrative produces a very different address: a violent conflict of fictional modes brings about a strong emotional response, willing the impossible, wishing for the consummation of the love affair even at the expense of plausibility itself. The initiation of a possible narrative 'chain' (a love affair) and the simultaneous withdrawal of the satisfactions possible within that 'chain' produces a situation of tension, of unrequited emotionality, that is very different from the position produced by the documentary mode of address. There is no possible point of unification of the discourses offered by the film at this point. Documentary and fictional narrative provide contradictory positions: harmony is posed in one, a harmony from a position of detached observation; frustration and disorder are posed in the other, these being produced by the refusal of the fiction's own initial premises to permit its resolution.

The architecture of the film is built from its attempt to resolve this contradiction between modes of address, between mastery and frustration. The film works to re-integrate these two modes, to produce a position of mastery with involvement, with pleasure. It is this contradiction between modes of address and their implication of the subject that motivates the opposition between the narrative real of the colour sequences (3, 5, 7, 8, 9, 10, 11, 12, 14, 15, 16, 18, 20, 22, 23) and the documentary real of the 'hallucination' sequences (4, 6, 13, 17, 19, 21,). This may seem a startling claim, since the whole of the central section of the film (7-12) is entirely in colour, and several times the heavenly messenger, Conductor 71, appears in the colour sequences. Nevertheless, it still remains true that the specification of the film's dislocations, the troubling of the initial harmony that it worries over, is centred around the 'lack of fit' between the discursive form of documentary and the discursive form of the fictional love story. The narrative turns on the contradiction between them, it constantly returns to the points where they conflict.

Each discourse, fiction and documentary, has a different 'internal economy': each form of containment of the heterogeneous is arranged differently. This can be expressed in a schematic way as each having ideas that are centralised and others which are marginalised or denied any real place. It has to be noted that, first, this is schematic because it ignores the processes of signification that produce these 'ideas', and, second, that these remarks apply only to the particular balance within the documentary and narrative forms at the time that *A Matter of Life and Death* was made. They are not universally applicable remarks. At this time, it seems that fiction centralised sexuality, individual psychology, the particularity of a situation between characters; and documentary, (then a recognisable mode, diffused massively during the war), centralised generality, exposition, broad concepts relating to social order. Fiction on the contrary resists generalisation, the discourses of society, social rather than psychological explanation; and documentary at this time resists sexuality, the centrality of the individual, the construction of a psychology addressed to the audience. Each of these discursive forms produces an effect of reality within its systematisation a centralised or marginal conceptions. Documentary sequences in this film have the status of a 'reality' just as the fictional ones. This sense of reality is an effect produced by the discursive form. The discourse constructs a position of intelligibility, a point of unity for the subject. The effect for the spectator is that of being addressed by reality, rather than being implicated in a discursive system. In this film, two discursive forms are offered, each with its own rather different arrangements and therefore rather different subject positions.

The central term of the differentiation between these two discursive forms is sexuality. Nowadays, this would no longer be a possible textual strategy: documentary is no longer a unitary discursive practice, and sexuality (the family, sexology etc.) have entered definitively within the concerns of expository film-making. Within *A Matter of Life and Death*, the differentiation is very clear. The monochrome sequences deal with organisation, with the harmonious order of the Other World, with social individuals each having a chosen place in that order. Sexuality emerges only at the edge of this world, and is repressed, e.g. Bob's relationship with the Angel is only briefly hinted at, and his attempt at conversation with her at the beginning of the trial is cut short by the arrival of the Judge (19). Monochrome itself has at this time certain definite connotations: those of the everyday, of 'reality as it is lived' (connotations that continue even to the Woodfall 'New Wave' films). Monochrome was the natural medium for serious subjects, for documentary: it was in no way considered inferior to colour. The colour sequences deal with very different ideas. Providing the bulk of the film's central sequences, the meanings they elaborate are more concerned with individuals, with psychology, with producing an awareness of complex inter-personal relations. Sexuality emerges as central, and the realisation of sexual significations takes place around the figure of June, through the film's concern to find an adequate position for her, though the constant emphasis on her gaze (her 'concern', her 'disbelief' etc.).

The centrality of sexuality to the difference between the monochrome and colour sequences is evident from the meanings that coalesce around the two characters who make a transition between the two worlds: Conductor 71 and Reeves. Reeves' sexual position is uncertain in the earlier sequences: he has an (unrequited) admiration for June (8); June senses the ambiguity of his attraction to Peter (10,11). His death removes this ambiguity, not only from the narrative but also from the character, as his role in the Other World is as uncomplicatedly patriarchal as the prosecutor Farlan's. Conductor 71 makes the opposite transition. He hardly appears in the Other World's social atmosphere (his longest monochrome appearance is alone with Peter on the escalator (13)), and his frivolity has a sexual edge, concerned with his image in a narcissistic way that is entirely untypical of the Other World's inhabitants. On earth, however, it makes sense: his admiration for June is undisguised, his dandyism complements an arbitrary display of his powers that is designed to intimidate Peter (11). He is more comfortable in the world (hence his famous remark: 'One is starved for Technicolor up there' (7)), his 'witty, decadent frivolity' (Durgnat) can exercise its sexual edge, display the refined sexual play that it is.

So the differentiation between the two forms that the film poses centres itself on sexuality. One discursive order resists the incursions of the sexual, the other gives them a centrality and devotes itself to the regulation and containment of sexuality where the other multiplies its expositions, its sense of order, its position of cool mastery in order to refuse sexuality. Initially, the film poses the documentary form as one of harmony, and then the fictional narrative form as the disruption. The love-story is all the more disruptive because it seems destined, by all the laws of narrative plausibility, to be unrequited. The film then settles into an elaboration of the conflicts between each mode by having them interrupt each other, make incursions into each other's equilibrium. If it weren't for Peter's case, the Other World would continue smoothly; if it weren't for the Other World's interventions, Peter and June's love affair would have no more than trivial problems. It is possible here to psychologise this difference of discursive modes, a difference centring on sexuality, and claim that it represents Peter's ambivalence towards a sexual involvement. The Other World then becomes Peter's own so-called 'unconscious', trying to draw him back from the kind of involvement that June represents. Yet there are very good reasons why this psychologising should not take place: it ignores several fundamental features of the film's system: the way in which the Other World sequences are in no way placed as 'subjective', but are usually taken as having a reality separate from Peter's imaginings; the way in which the definition of sexuality involves Reeves and June rather than Peter. Firstly, the sexuality that June 'represents' is not certain or fixed, it is constantly worried over by the film. Sexuality has no precise form, no exact contours, and the attempt to give it definite characteristics, to contain it for the viewing subject, is one of the major tasks for virtually any narrative film. Secondly, despite the film's initiating caption (1), reviewers do not accord an absolute subjective status to the Other World sequences, indeed it is very difficult to do so whilst watching the film: the hold of their discursive mode over the view is too strong, they create an effect of reality. Both of these ideas need detailed elaboration as they are central to the film's working: the signification of sexuality; the different subject-positions involved in the documentary and narrative fiction modes.

The problem of definition of June's sexuality revolves around the question of whether she is the object or the subject of desires. Seq. 3 begins with mutual incomprehension and impatience: June 'can't understand' Peter; Peter is exasperated that she wants to know his position. With seq. 7, the suspension of time during Conductor 71, appearance freezes June into an object, an object for the admiration of the Conductor, a passive and unresponsive being for Peter. This is the first of two crucial moments where June is reduced to immobility, to pure objecthood, the other being seq. 18. This first freezing is followed by June doubting (close-up of puzzled expression) the truth of Peter's hallucination. She pays for this doubt: she is eradicated from both Peter's and our vision, when, in a subjective shot from Peter's position, she is obscured by a haze, and is only restored after a moment of panic on Peter's part. Thus one moment in the definition of June's position is that of pure objecthood, that of eradication from the image at the moment that she displays an independence from Peter's thinking.

This moment of objecthood is not the primary definition of June's sexuality. Peter's 'illness' means that he slides out of the sexual, his desire for June (once established as being the desire of 'I, Peter' for the object June) is taken for granted. During the rest of the film June makes a transition from being the object of desire to becoming an active, desiring subject. The second time that she is frozen by the intervention of Conductor 71 (seq. 18), her active desire produces a tear on her cheek, 'the only real evidence we have.' Although June's identity is still posed exclusively in terms of her sexuality, it is notable how it becomes increasingly active and desiring, and as a consequence, the film is lead to refuse certain conceivable activities for her: she scarcely nurses Peter, for instance; this function devolves far more on Reeves. June's transition from being a passive object to participating actively in the play of desire (from Peter's 'my defence' to his 'we won') is effected through a further definition of June's sexuality in relation to Reeves, taking Peter as the (frozen) object of *their* desire.

June's initial relationship with Reeves is posed as friendship on her part, unrequited desire on his. (As he sees her in his camera obscura he says 'Here's June: "She walks in beauty like the night," only she's cycling and the sun's out' (8)). A rivalry between them for Peter begins with Reeves revealing that he admires Peter's poetry, where June does not even know that he is a poet. The sequence (10) continues with Reeves interrogating Peter, and June looking on (shots emphasise her reactions as the conversation takes new, disturbing, turns). Moments of particular tension are: (a) the interchange: Reeves: 'What was the cause of your father's death?' Peter: 'Same as mine;' (b) the test of Peter's vision, at the end of which June remarks: 'When the two of you have quite finished admiring that girl's legs;' (c) Reeves: 'Do you believe in the survival of the human personality after death?' Peter: 'I thought you'd read my verses;' June: 'I've never really thought about it;' Reeves: 'I don't know, I've thought about it too much;' (d) the interchange about tea-time: Reeves grumpily remarks that he always has tea at 4.30, and the 5.00 tea at June's air-base is 'past my time.' It is impossible at this length, without the use of stills, to illustrate how these interchanges become charged with a particular sexual signification: it is a matter of concentration on June's reactions at certain moments, of tone of voice — of *mise en scene.* This explication risks imprecision and the imposition of too thin a meaning, but it still has to risk the assertion that a rivalry is developing between Reeves and June, a rivalry of a more or less sexual nature for possession of Peter. It increasingly defines June's sexuality as that of an active desire, and it motivates her aggression towards Reeves in the next sequence (11). Here, she is playing table-tennis with Reeves as Peter is asleep; she asks why Peter is asleep, Reeves answers that he's given him a tablet, and he will wake at a specified time. June challenges him: how can he possibly know that? Reeves says he knows his patient. June responds with a sudden aggressive burst 'But do you really know him?' Reeves response is defensive: 'Are we playing table tennis or are we not?', which June mimics. She deliberately misses a shot so as to lose the game, and continues the conversation. Reeves says he finds Peter fascinating. 'So do I.' 'Not biologically,' he replies, 'but medically.' They then discuss Peter, standing in front of the supine object of their fascination: a reversal of the situation where June is frozen for the contemplation of the men. From this point, June and Reeves reach an understanding over Peter, and June's sexuality has gained a certain clarity of definition. These two sequences (10 and 11) are immensely complex and long (10:7 mins; 11:10 mins), and contain in addition to the above, many of the plays with the question of perception for which the film is well known. It is not possible here to analyse the mutual articulation of these ideas (sexuality, perception) across these sequences; it is a matter only of signalling the way in which the film is systematised. Sexuality provides the main point of differentiation between the two discursive forms employed in the film, and the sexuality of June, the central female character, provides the main problem of definition. It now remains to examine the discursive modes themselves in the light of the above claim, that the film's disruption of an initial order is posed in across the lack of fit between two discursive forms.

Documentary and fictional narrative involve rather different positions for the viewing subject; different positions of truth are posed within them. Documentary addresses itself to judgment, to the spectator as adjudicator; the point of truth is that of the logic, the systematic organisation of the information proffered by the film, information that is itself concerned with order, with organisation, with the social. Fictional narrative implicates the subject in a work of containing the heterogeneous, with producing signification from the flux of a disrupted order. Each holds the spectator in a position of separation and involvement with the image ('It's only a film,' yet 'It's offered to me'), but documentary offers itself to judgment, where the fictional narrative offers itself to 'involvement,' that is to a process whereby psychological similarities are recognised with the characters, similarities which are then invested with certain demands for the realisation of generalised phantasies.

It is usually the case with films which pose two different discursive modes that one is strictly subordinated to the other. One is given the status of an insert of some kind, the subordinated discourse is anchored into the main one by definite forms of transition (e.g. dissolves linking dreams/visions to a close-up/dolly into the dreamer). Yet here there is no anchoring of one discourse into another: the forms of transition pose, in various ways, a continuum between each form (rose gaining its colour (6-7), dissolve on voice similarity (13-14). The only truly subjective transition is Seqs. 16-17, which inaugurates the final argument in the Other World which will decide the case. Despite the opening title placing the Other World as Peter's hallucination, therefore, the film itself makes it difficult to maintain this subjectivisation. The viewer is given two realities, two truths, two worlds. The film operates on the disjunction between the two worlds, posed in two discursive forms.

Being a Powell/Pressburger film, it is not content to leave this disjuncture between two subject-positions lying unelaborated: the film does more than just pose a documentary and a narrative fiction mode of address, and leave it at that. Persistently, the implications of this disjunction are examined: the film contains a series of demonstrations of different forms of cinematic vision and representation. Some of these moments are spectacular — in the sense that they disturb the expected relation of visuality, providing an excess of visual pleasure and an unsettling awareness of the film as signification rather than presentation of the real. I will only catalogue these moments, indicating something of their context: again, it is impossible in this space to examine the way that these disruptions articulate with the scenes around them.

(1) The simplest moment (an affront to some critics), where Conductor 71

arrives on earth and announces: 'One is starved for Technicolor up there.' (seq. 70). Powell's comment is enough: 'Another thing I was pleased about, I was able to step outside the conventions . . . (it) is a pure inside joke. That was a plus for me to be able to do a thing like that in a big film and not a comedy' (Gough-Yates p.10).

(2) A more complex situation: in 5, Peter has just been washed ashore in the strange dawn light on a deserted beach. He finds first a 'Keep Out' notice, confirming for the audience that he has indeed stayed on earth as the Other World administration had suspected in the previous sequence. Peter does not know this, however. He comes upon an extraordinary sight: a naked young shepherd boy, playing a flute whilst his goats and dog surround him. The image, lit with the thin clear light of early morning, is bizarre enough, but where the audience take it as bizarre, Peter reads it as cliche: the Arcadian angel. He asks where he has to report, and the boy quite naturally directs him to the air station. Through the irony of the disparity between Peter's interpretation and the audience's (a reversal of the normal presentation of the bizarre: here it is 'natural' for the character, bizarre for the audience), the meaning of an image has been demonstrated to depend on interpretation.

(3) This is taken further in 10: use is made of the standard device for a fiction film to comment upon the nature of representation: the presentation of a stage-play. Here, it is a rehearsal of a comic scene from *Midsummer Night's Dream*, Bottom's lines about how 'Wall' is to be represented, taking realist conventions to their logical and absurd conclusion. These lines are presented twice (emphasis), the second time with a new dimension: the American private playing Bottom has the opportunity to use the business to hit his officer several times. Hence, not only representation involving pretence, conventions of depiction, but also the acting-out of fantasies, at least on the part of the performers.

The next three incidents are more directly concerned with modes of looking, of the peculiar forms of looking that cinema involves.

(4) In seq. 8, Reeves' camera obscura is demonstrated, through a series of shots which give details of its mechanism, its effects, and a conversation between Reeves and June about the mode of seeing that it involves. After an establishing shot (Reeves and the projection table), the camera obscura image occupies the screen: an effect very similar to a long panning crane shot is gained. This is followed by a shot through the projection system itself. The conversation about the device with June emphasises the power which this unobserved observation can give the doctor: June accuses him of surveying his kingdom; he says it often provides vital information for his diagnoses. He then describes its effect: 'You can see clearly and all at once, as in a poet's eye': it is a totalising vision, seeing everything unobserved, a kind of voyeurism.

(5) In seq. 11, a direct comparison is made between the vision of a moving camera and the vision of a moving eye. The game of table-tennis is

first shot with the camera panning wildly back and forth between the players, following the ball. The effect is shocking, disturbing as the pans are so fast. After June and Reeves have worked through their rivalry over Peter, the next game is shot more placidly and conventionally in long shot: the viewer's eye rather than the camera follows the ball from side to side across the screen. The difference is immediately apparent: the effect of a moving camera is radically different from the effect of an eye moving across an image. The play between the disturbing and the more reassuring shots runs across the rivalry between June and Reeves, each intensifying the other's effect across the scene: rivalry becomes division of interest as disturbing pans settle into a more habitual form of looking.

(6) Seqs 12 and 16 both contain a dolly shot through the army hospital's corridor. The purpose of the first is only to cue in, to provide a point of comparison and reference for the second. The second is subjective, that is shot from the point of view of Peter lying on a stretcher. Again a comparison. The subjective sequence goes further, by providing in the operating threatres a series of alternations between subjective and general (narrational) shots. Finally, a transition is provided: the camera executes a $90°$ pan and dolly shot so that it begins with Peter's profile and ends in the place of his head. The oxygen mask descends in front of the image, disappearing beneath it; a brief cutaway to Peter looking then provides the transition to the effect of the image being 'behind' one eye. The eyelids close, we are inside Peter's head. The audacity of this sequence is its literal-mindedness. It takes the notion of a subjective camera to its superb conclusion. It is the one possibility that Montgomery's *The Lady in the Lake* (made at virtually the same time) completely neglects: in that film when the camera-hero closes his eyes to be kissed, the screen merely goes dark.

Rather than isolated moments, these particular events are logical and coherent developments of the system of the film. They operate largely by comparison or by repetition-with-difference, and they emphasise the way in which the attitude of the spectator can be remarkably different within the space of one film, and, more, how these differing attitudes can conflict, yet are bound within a certain mode of representation (voyeurism, the playing of roles). A discussion of the nature of representation (not so unusual in films, e.g. *My Darling Clementine's* drunk Shakespearean.) is carried on not only within the conventional terms — a representation represented within the film — but also, more radically, addressing itself directly to the audience in the form of comparative exercises in 'how you see.'

Thus *A Matter of Life and Death* can be seen to work by exploiting the disjunction between two discursive modes which propose rather different positions of intelligibility. The film opens out, follows the repercussions of this initiation, by centring its difference on the problem of definition of sexuality, a term to which one of the discourses offers a marked resistance. In doing so, it is involved in the constant negotiation between the different subject-positions proffered by each discourse, and this work produces across the film a series of events which examine the nature of

101

representation, resolutely refusing any equation between camera and eye, between image and real.

This work continues, strictly speaking, until the last sequence, but the reintegration of the elements that are posited initially as being in contradiction is carried out in a rather different mode. An argument is presented between the proponents of each discursive mode: Reeves for the love-story, Farlan for the documentary of the Law and Order of the Other World. The argument has no arbiter deciding which point has been won or lost: it is addressed to the audience, for their arbitration. It is over the definition of the case of Peter Carter: the Law's representative arguing for the maximum number of social divisions, centring on the difference of nationality between Peter and June, a difference which it is claimed will make real love impossible. Reeves on the other hand has only the fact of real love to argue with, and attempts to demolish Farlan's divisions and distinctions as prejudice that love could overcome. The jury is demonstrated to be prejudiced against Britain because of the crimes of imperialism, and America is finally demonstrated to be the place where these old national antagonisms will be overcome: a nation composed of other nations. Thus the argument is effectively won at this point, as Reeves' contention about the power of love is demonstrated in the composition of the American 'nation.' Love and justice on the one side, order and the law on the other have found a synthesis, yet this synthesis, posed in the terms of an abstract argument, are not enough for the film. The effectivity of each term and the form of their synthesis has to be demonstrated for characters of the narrative. The documentary mode has reached its conclusion in the argument, but the fictional narrative demands a different form of resolution. Its terms are rather different: it is a matter of the rights of the individual against the law of the universe, 'The rights of the uncommon man must always be respected.' The resolution, finally, is uneasy. Law has to make concessions to love because, in some way, love is the basis of Heavenly law. However, the fact remains that the fictional narrative reaches its desired re-ordering. Peter is reunited with his chess-book (the last element is fitted into the new ordering), he and June have won, together. They have moved from being voices searching for each other across the night air, through being desiring male and desired female object, to being united: 'We', the film's culminating emphasis as daylight comes streaming through the window.

This analysis has demonstrated to some extent the terms in which *A Matter* works. That is to say, it has shown that the work of the film is one of producing a narrative from the dislocation between two discourses, a dislocation that takes place on the ground of sexuality, and produces across the film a series of examinations of the nature of cinema as a particular kind of event for a spectator who adopts a special relation to it.

It could be objected that this tells nothing about the film, its 'content', its 'message.' All of which is true, given that such an analysis conceives of the film outside these terms. 'Content' and 'message' become hopelessly imprecise: according to the above analysis, the film is 'about' representation, the relation spectator/cinematic text, sexuality, law v. love, documentary v. narrative, realism, the nature of heaven and earth, discourses and subjects, table-tennis — any number of things. However, some claim a definite content and message for the film, as Raymond Durgnat demonstrates: '*A Matter of Life and Death* is generally taken as an extravaganza, a vague, eccentric, enjoyable contraption advocating closer ties with the USA. But the politics of this "Halfway Heaven" are far more precise. They express the perennial Tory criticisms of the Socialist Utopia — that is, the Welfare State . . . Critics of the time felt that Heaven must stand for Hitler's "New Order," his arbitrary totalitarian world. The Robsons drew many parallels, even down to the detail that Himmler means Heaven in German. But surely this heavenly city isn't bestial enough for Nazism. It isn't even malicious, merely coldly efficient. And the film's preoccupation is not with Britain's survival in war, but with her survival in peace. . . This Heaven is a futurist Utopia. It's planned society. It's machine-like. . . Heaven's values are those of the collectivity (as opposed to the selfless individualism of romantic love). Planned, bureaucratic, idealistic, totalitarian, colourless, theorectic — all these are words Tories like to use of Socialism.' (Durgnat pp.29-30).

It should be clear from the analysis that it provides an exposition of how the film is capable of producing all these 'interpretations' of its 'content' and its ideological position. It claims that all these interpretations are produced through a mechanism (a film) which is more complex than any of these interpretations. The interpretations aim to fix the movement of the film, to tie it down and avoid its irritating irridescences.

Yet it is not enough to propose a simple relationship between this analysis and statements of supposed content (analysis: 'Here is the mechanism that produces various interpretations'). The analysis reveals something that the notion of 'content' represses: that the film is centrally concerned with the problems of representation, and with producing a scepticism about notions of realism. It produces two realities, realities that are the effects of differing discursive forms. It then intensifies the awareness of the discursive production of realities by working on the point of greatest disparity between them (the conception of sexuality), and by confronting the audience throughout with the discursive reality of the alleged 'real' that they are 'witnessing'. What the film does, then, is to question the very basis of the analysis of films in terms of 'content' that is, the effect of reality which is usually produced silently through the operation of one discursive form with one position of intelligibility and truth. Analysis of content, effect of reality: silent partners, conspirators in British narrative cinema and orthodox film criticism alike. A conspiracy that, over thirty years ago, Powell and Pressburger were concerned to criticise.

BIBLIOGRAPHY

A short list of the principal theoretical writing upon which this piece draws.

Roland Barthes *S/Z*, (Paris, 1970).

Jean Collet *et al Lectures du Film* (Paris 1975).

Rosalind Coward, John Ellis *Language and Materialism*, (London 1977).

Stephen Heath *The Nouveau Roman*, (London 1972). 'Film and System: Terms of Analysis,' *Screen* v. 16 nos. 1, 2.   Narrative Space,' *Screen* v. 17 no. 3.

Colin MacCabe 'Principles of Realism and Pleasure,' *Screen* v. 17 no. 3.

Christian Metz 'The Imaginary Signifier', *Screen* v. 16 no. 2.

Laura Mulvey 'Visual Pleasure and Narrative Cinema,' *Screen* v. 16 no. 3.

Bill Nichols 'Documentary Theory and Practice', *Screen* v. 17 no. 4.

Paul Willemen 'Voyeurism, the Look and Dwoskin', *Afterimage*, no. 6, Summer 1976.

4 *Blimp*, Churchill and the State

Ian Christie

> Lady Astor was bound to acknowledge that England was now being saved by its
> Blimps and its Blimpish character. I did not get far enough to say what I really think,
> which is that Churchill's strength and the reason he refuses to give ground anywhere
> is because he himself is a Blimpish character who has a very high intelligence and
> knowledge of history on top of it.
>
> General Raymond E Lee, *The London Observer* (1940) [1]

It is no secret that *The Life and Death of Colonel Blimp* (hereafter *Blimp)*
provoked serious official hostility and was for a time refused normal
export permission. Powell and Pressburger recall warnings from Jack
Beddington, head of the Film Section of the Ministry of Information, and
from the Minister, Brendan Bracken. The fact that it was then severely cut
for American release and subsequent circulation in Britain has also led to
speculation about covert Government censorship. But until the recent
discovery of a correspondence file detailing Churchill's campaign to
suppress *Blimp,* there was no conclusive evidence of interference. Now the
evidence is available and is reproduced here for the first time, along with
some interpolated material. [2] Coincidentally, the complete 'text' of the
film, which was eventually reduced to about two-thirds of its original
length, is now available for the first time since 1943, thanks to restoration
by the National Film Archive. [3] The following presentation and commentary attempts to reassess the issues raised by the film and its impact in the
light of these developments.

1. The Attempted Suppression of Blimp

The Life and Death of Colonel Blimp was written as an original screenplay
by Emeric Pressburger sometime in early 1942 (see *Chronicle*). At this
stage, it was called 'The Life and Death of Sugar Candy' (after Clive
Candy's nickname), and the title page of the script held by the British Film
Institute Library indicates that it was to be made between July and
September 1942, with Lawrence Olivier as Candy. The title was not
changed until after shooting had begun, apparently as a result of contacts
with David Low, the creator of the Blimp cartoon character. According to
Powell: [4]

> Then we ran into trouble with the Ministry of Information, who read the script and
> thought it was defeatist — they never did appreciate the fact that as an artist or
> storyteller you have to show what's bad before you can show what's good. You can't go

out saying we're bound to be all right because we're British. You've got to show all the bad bits first, which propagandists never do. They said: 'We don't think you should make this film. You can't have Laurence Olivier'. 'You're going to stop us making it?' 'Oh no, we're not going to stop you. After all this is a democracy, but we advise you not to make it and you can't have Olivier, because he's in the Fleet Air Arm and we're not going to release him to play your Colonel Blimp.' So we came out of the MoI and Emeric said to me, 'What shall we do' and I said, 'We'll play Roger Livesey . . .' We had a huge premiere that Churchill came to, but he didn't like it. He sent out a lot of memos saying 'Disgraceful'.

In fact, Churchill already knew of the film while it was still being shot: the PRO file PREM 4 14/15 opens with a memorandum from the Secretary of State for War, dated 8 September 1942:

PRIME MINISTER
I attach, as directed, a note on the Blimp film which is in course of being produced and which I think it of the utmost importance to get stopped.

P G[rigg]

The Life and Death of Colonel Blimp

1. The theme of the film is, according to the producer, the struggle of the junior officer in the Army against the obstructiveness of the Blimps at the top and his subsequent metamorphosis into a Blimp himself. The film begins with a collision between a young officer of today and Major-General Clive Candy, aged 66. The occasion is a Home Guard exercise for the defence of London. The young man starts his attack several hours before the exercise is due to begin and surprises the opposing general while the latter is still in his Turkish bath. This is supposed to be an example of ruthless initiative. The film then goes back to 1902 when the General himself was a subaltern with a similar intolerance of his elders and impetuous enough to embarrass the British Embassy in Germany by fighting a duel with a German officer. Then it traces his progress across the years in various parts of the British Empire, and so to the war of 1914-1918 and the post-war years. In the war of 1914-1918 Candy's playing the game according to the rules is contrasted with the greater realism of a South-African officer. Candy's attitude between the wars is a lack of comprehension as to why the Germans cannot realise that they were fairly and squarely beaten and there is no reason why they should not make and remain friends. A confused love interest (with three different women) also complicates the story at various intervals.

2. The producer claims that the film is intended as a tribute to the toughness and keeness of the new Army in Britain and shows how far they have progressed from the Blimpery of the pre-war Army. From this point of view he urges that it would be valuable propaganda for the USA and the Dominions because in showing that we are conscious of any faults which we may possess, we are telling the rest of the world that the faults are being eliminated.

3. The War Office have refused to give their support to the film in any way on the ground that it would give the Blimp conception of the Army officer a new lease of life at a time when it is already dying from inanition. Whatever the film makes of the spirit of the young soldier of today, the fact remains that it focuses attention on an imaginary type of Army officer which has become an object of ridicule to the general public. In the opening scheme (*sic*) Candy is shown as Blimp himself complete with towel and everything. Whatever it may do elsewhere the film has made a character built up by twenty years of brilliant cartooning into a figure of fun, and there is the inescapable suggestion that such a man is a type or at any rate an example of those who have risen to high command in the Army in the period preceeding this war.

4. There is the further objection that the Germans in the film are depicted as stiff and over-regimented in peace and as little more than very intense realists in war. The thug element in the make-up of the German soldier is ignored and indeed the suggestion is that if we were exactly like the Germans we should be better soldiers.

5. As stated above, the War Office have refused all facilities for the film, but production is still going on at Denham and the Minister of Information knows of no way in which it can be stopped. Steps have been taken, however, to bring home to the person financing the film the fact that it is viewed with disfavour by the War Office and that no Army facilities will be available. Whether anything will come of this indirect approach is at present uncertain.

*

Prime Minister's Personal Minute M.357/2
MINISTER OF INFORMATION
Pray propose to me the measures necessary to stop this foolish production before it gets any further. I am not prepared to allow propaganda detrimental to the morale of the Army, and I am sure the Cabinet will take all necessary action. Who are the people behind it?

W S C[hurchill]   10 September 1942

*

Ministry of Information
PRIME MINISTER

The Colonel Blimp Film

Your minute No. M357/2

This film is being produced by Archer Films Ltd, a company entirely owned by Mr Michael Powell and Mr Emmerich Pressburger. I understand that the production is financed by General Film Distributors Ltd, the head of which is Mr Joseph Rank.

The Ministry of Information has no power to suppress the film. We have been unsuccessful in discouraging it by the only means open to us: that is, by withholding Government facilities for its production.

I am advised that in order to stop it the Government would need to assume powers of a very far-reaching kind. These could hardly be less than powers to suppress all films, even those based on imaginary stories, on grounds not of their revealing information to the enemy but of their expressing harmful or misguided opinions. Moreover it would be illogical for the Government to insist on a degree of control over films which it does not exercise over other means of expression, such as books or newspaper articles. Nothing less, therefore, than the imposition of a compulsory censorship of opinion upon all means of expression would meet the case, and I am certain that this could not be done without provoking infinite protest.

If you or the War Office were to let it be known to Mr Rank that it is your wish that the film should be dropped, I feel sure that it would be dropped. But I do not think that any approach of this kind should come from the Ministry of Information. As the Department responsible for Censorship, the Ministry is liable to be suspected of abusing its Censorship powers and requests from us frequently meet with a resistance which they would not encounter if made by a Department that has no connection with Censorship.

B[rendan] B[racken] 15 September 1942

*

Prime Minister's Personal Minute M.381/2
MINISTER OF INFORMATION
We should act not on the grounds of 'expressing harmful or misguided opinions' but on the perfectly precise point of 'undermining the discipline of the Army'. You and the Secretary of State should bring the matter before the Cabinet on Monday [*marginal note:* 'This was done'.] when I have no doubt any special authority you may require will be given you. The Ministry of Information is the seat of the Censorship,

and consequently you are the channel for any Cabinet decision on the subject.

W S C   17 September 1942

*

War Cabinet 126 (42). Monday 21 September 1942

7. The Secretary of State for War said that a film about 'Colonel Blimp' was being made. Facilities had been asked for from the War Office. These had been refused, on the ground that the films was likely to bring ridicule upon the Army. The producers had, nevertheless, proceeded with the making of the film, which was now at an advanced stage.

There was no existing Defence Regulation under which the film could be suppressed. He understood that the Minister of Information was averse from taking the very wide powers which would be necessary to stop this film.

More recently, however, an approach had been made to the financier who was backing the film, who had agreed that, when the film had reached the 'rough cut stage' it should be seen by representatives of the War Office and the Ministry of Information; and if they took the view that the film was undesirable he would arrange for it to be withdrawn.

General agreement was expressed with the view that it was impossible to allow a film to be produced which was liable to undermine the discipline of the Army; and satisfaction was expressed that this could be achieved by the friendly arrangement outlined by the Secretary of State for War.

*

War Cabinet 67 (43). 10 May 1943.

4. The Secretary of State for War said that the film had now been seen by representatives of the War Office and the Ministry of Information, who took the view that it was unlikely to attract much attention or to have any undesirable consequences on the discipline of the Army. In the circumstances, he had reached the conclusion that the right plan was to allow the film to be shown.

The War Cabinet — Endorsed this view.

The following month an item appeared in the Diary of the London *Evening Standard* (28.6.43) which looks suspiciously like an attempt to satisfy public curiosity about what was becoming an embarrassment to the Ministry of Information.

Whitehall has decided — whether officially or unofficially is not quite clear, but the decision will be effective — that the film of Colonel Blimp is not for the present to be exported for exhibition abroad. I am able to give what I am assured is the inside story of this ban.

Mr Churchill was at the first night of the film [the World Premiere was at the Odeon Leicester Square on 10 June] and seems to have formed some pretty definite opinions about it. He talked to his colleagues in the Cabinet and to Whitehall officials. Then almost every Government department sent delegations to view the film and gave their own impressions.

When all the reports were in, they were solemnly collated and examined. Then some highup made the decision that it would not be advisable to let the film go out as representing the British Army.

Public attention has mainly been focussed on the picture of the British officer drawn in the film, and of his extreme conservatism. But the veto decision was (not) made on this point at all. It was made on a point that few people would have thought of.

In the film a young Army officer wins a victory over Home Guard Colonel Blimp by fighting a 'battle' some hours before the appointed zero hour. This, says Whitehall, would advertise abroad that we countenance the ethics of the Japs at Pearl Harbour!

Thus are great decisions made.

Ministry of Information
PRIME MINISTER
Mr Arthur Rank, who is Chairman of Gaumont British, is asking if this Ministry can give him a definite decision about the export of the film 'Colonel Blimp'. So far we have been withholding the facilities for export by air which would normally be accorded to any British film of standing.

Is it still your wish that this film should not go abroad? We have no legal power to stop it, and indeed the statements appearing in the newspapers saying that it has been banned probably only serve to advertise it.

My advice is that the film should be allowed to go. At a time when the prestige of the British fighting man stands higher in the world than it has ever done, I think the circulation of this evident fantasy presents no dangers at all. But if you still feel strongly that it should not go abroad, I will try to find means of continuing our illegal ban.

B B   9 July 1943

*

Prime Minister's Personal Minute M.459/3
MINISTER OF INFORMATION
I think you should certainly stop it going abroad as long as you possibly can.

W S C   11 July 1943

*

Ministry of Information
PRIME MINISTER
You asked in your Minute No. M.459/3 that this Ministry should stop the film 'Colonel Blimp' from going abroad as long as we possibly could.

This we have so far managed to do by the unorthodox expedient of refusing the normal facilities for transport abroad by air. But even if we were able to persist in this expedient, we could not either by legal or illegal action prevent the film from going abroad by other means.

We have now had an official letter from Mr. Rank, the producer of the film, informing us that he would to show it in America and in the Empire. As the film is so boring I cannot believe it will do any harm abroad to anyone except the company which made it. And as this Ministry has no reason to protect the company from the
A consequences of its follies, I should propose to tell Mr Rank that he may make his own arrangements accordingly.

B B   23 July 1943

*

Prime Minister's Personal Minute M.523/3
MINISTER OF INFORMATION
I do not agree with this surrender. Will you please discuss the matter with me. If necessary we must take more powers.

W S C   25 July 1943

*

Ministry of Information
PRIME MINISTER
Your Minute No. M.523/3 of 25 July.

The word 'surrender' is not in our vocabulary! As a result of our illegal ban on this wretched film 'Colonel Blimp' has received a wonderful advertisement from the Government. It is now enjoying an extensive run in the suburbs and in all sorts of places there are notices — 'See the banned film!'

If we had left that dull film alone it would probably have proved an unprofitable undertaking, but by the time the Government have finished with it here is no knowing what profits it will have earned.

B B   5 August 1943

[Slip headed with Prime Minister's seal. Handwritten]
Mr Rowan (Prime Minister's secretary)
Please see 'A' [see 23 July above]. A reply to Mr Rank from Mr Bracken is now outstanding; Mr Bracken however is in no hurry and told me not to telegraph about it.

[initials indecipherable]
(in Churchill's handwriting) Leave it for the time being.

*

PRIME MINISTER
I am not clear about your minute 'Leave it for the time being'. As you will see from Flag A, Mr Bracken has received an official letter from Mr. Rank informing him that Mr. Rank would like to show 'Colonel Blimp' in America and the Empire. One this Mr. Bracken minuted:
'And as the Ministry has no reason for trying to protect the company from the consequences of its follies, I should propose to tell Mr. Rank that he may make his own arrangements accordingly.'
May I now be informed that you approve this?

T L R[owan]   15 August 1943
[Churchill's handwriting] No. I am obstructing. Leave it till Mr. B arrives.

*

MOST SECRET CYPHER TELEGRAM
From: Air Ministry. To: Quadrant (Ministry of Information).   19 August 1943
Following for Sendall from Hodge.
We have had a further letter from Mr. Rank requesting facilities for the export of the film 'Colonel Blimp'. He says it has broken all previous box-office records for the Odeon circuit of cinemas. In view of this it is becoming practically impossible to maintain our illegal ban. May we have directions?

*

MOST SECRET CYPHER TELEGRAM
From: Quadrant. To: War Cabinet Offices London. 25 August 1943
Following for Hodge, Ministry of Information from Sendall.
Approval to release 'Blimp' has now been secured.

On the following day, the Executive Board of the Ministry of Information discussed *Blimp* (IBF 1 73).

FILM: THE LIFE AND DEATH OF COLONEL BLIMP
Mr Gates reported that the general objections which had been raised to the export of this film, with which Mr. Rank had courteously complied, had now been withdrawn. He inquired whether any special objections now remained. Mr. Grubb recalled that exception had been taken to one or two sequences in the film by certain regional specialists; and Mr. Gates was invited to consider whether these should be represented to Mr. Rank.

The final document in the Blimp file is a letter from Sendall of the Ministry of Information to the Prime Minister's secretary.

Ministry of Information
21 September 1943
Dear Rowan,
I am returning your file about the release of 'Colonel Blimp' which somehow or other came into my hands while we were in America.

As you know, the Prime Minister finally authorised Mr. Bracken to withdraw his
ban on the export of this film.
Yours sincerely,
B C Sendall
[handwritten] I didn't; but P.A./T L R 22.9

What conclusions can be drawn from this record of bureaucratic
obstruction and inept bullying? On one level, it provides further evidence
of Churchill's autocratic control over all aspects of the war machinery; and
it sheds some light on the still inadequately documented working of the
Ministry of Information. Indirectly it also demonstrated how far Powell
and Pressburger had deviated from a semi-official consensus on the
acceptable forms of wartime propaganda. Regrettably, in the absence of a
full-scale examination of WW2 propaganda policy in relation to both the
'state apparatus' and the relatively autonomous agencies of cinema,
journalism, publishing, broadcasting, etc, the following annotations to the
Churchill/*Blimp* correspondence must remain tentative and fragmentary.

2. Censorship: Formal and Informal

Rather than consider what 'effects' censorship has on individual texts, the
crucial question should be: how is censorship internalised or accommo-
dated within the practice of a specific system of production and
distribution? (An equally important question, not to be pursued here, is
the effect censorship of one medium has on adjacent media: thus, for
instance, the differences between what 'can be shown' on film and on
television; or the comparison and relation between visual and verbal
taboos at any one time). In the British cinema, as is well known, the
exercise of censorship is peculiarly divided and displaced. While technical,
legal responsibility rests with local government authorities, the executive
responsibility is vested in a body financed by and (indirectly) regulated by
the production and distrubition sectors of the industry: the British Board
of Film Censors (BBFC). In theory, the autonomy of this body ensures its
impartiality; but it also allows a degree of 'slippage' in relations between
producers, distributors, exhibitors and local authorities, so that controversy tends to remain localised and does not provoke public debate on
the criteria of censorship. Another important feature of the British
self-regulating system is the extent to which the BBFC is able to influence
production and negotiate trends with producers and distributors. Far
from being a passive arbiter of acceptability, it can be seen as an active
promoter of consensus.

Immediately before the outbreak of WW2, there was a considerable
flurry of activity around the emergent Ministry of Information to set up a
'security censorship' procedure, which would deal with material for
domestic and foreign exhibition.[5] The Ministry of Information Film
Division soon declared its policy: 'It is unnecessary for us to consider, at
the moment, the censorship of ordinary interest or feature films.' (29.9.39).

The apparent rationale being that these were fictional and therefore, by definition, could not breach security. And when, as a result of confusion in the early months of the war, the BBFC introduced a special export certificate, a senior official of the Ministry of Information was 'horrified' to see the phrase *'and complies with the requirements of the Ministry of Information'* on the new certificate. He observed that this would suggest the Ministry 'has tampered with the film from a propaganda standpoint' (*loc cit*). 'Security censorship', therefore, was to be secret, functional, ideologically neutral; carried on behind the facade of normal BBFC certification.

The official position — and its unofficial side — are seen in operation in another exchange from the Ministry of Information files. In 1943, Conservative Central Office wrote to the Minister to alert him to the imminent arrival of *Mission to Moscow*, and American feature film directed by Michael Curtiz, made as part of the officially-sponsored pro-Soviet campaign. The letter was addressed to Brendan Bracken and appealed to him as a fellow-Conservative: 'Left-wing elements will make the most of the film in attacking our Party . . . I should be grateful if you could have a word in the appropriate quarter' (24.5.43). Bracken wrote in reply: 'This Ministry has no power to censor films of this description. We exercise no political censorship and we can only have things cut out on security grounds . . . If we find it objectionable we shall tell [the distributors] so, though we cannot do more than pass on to them our opinion' (28.5.34 *loc cit*).

The history of *Blimp* indicates that the Ministry could do rather more than 'pass on their opinions'. Powell recalls that they were advised directly by the Minister not to proceed with the film — but also assured that there was no formal ban![6] The ensuing publicity around the export 'ban' must have caused concern in the Ministry, hinting as it did at a clandestine political censorship. Presumably the *Evening Standard* diary item was the result of a clumsy official attempt to divert public speculation by producing a consensus 'justification' for the ban — thereby admitting that there was one. Characteristically, the British establishment preferred to disguise its political practice behind an appearance of bland informality.

3. Churchill and 'National Unity'

Winston Churchill's role in the attempted suppression of *Blimp* invites particular comment, especially since this is not the only instance on record of his direct interference. In his autobiography, Michael Balcon cites two Ealing productions which provoked Churchill's personal intervention. In the case of *Ships With Wings*, a somewhat romantic story concerning the Fleet Air Arm, Churchill 'had seen the film over the weekend and was insisting that the release should be held up, if not cancelled altogether, on the grounds that it would cause "alarm and despondency".'[7] Subsequently, Churchill left the final decision to the First Sea Lord who, in fact, 'saw no reason why the film should not be shown.' Balcon continues: 'I suppose the Prime Minister had no powers to stop the film but I would not have cared to put his authority to the test.' In the following year, Balcon had a similar experience with *Next of Kin*, made — rather ironically — at the request of the Director of Military Training to emphasise the importance of security precautions. Again Churchill saw the film privately and wanted its release delayed, supposedly because it showed an operation similar to Dieppe and might distress relatives of those killed in that engagement. But a military jury decided that it should be shown and it went on to become a considerable commercial success.

Charles Barr's comments on *Next of Kin* suggest why Churchill may have found it so disturbing:

> 'I've always thought if I wanted a nice cushy job I'd come to England as a German spy,' the security officer warns the army unit to which he is sent at the start of the film. Abundantly bearing him out, *Next of Kin* remains extremely disquieting in the way it works on its audience to show the dangers behind the familiar laziness bound up with niceness (the gentlemanly way officers refrain from questioning too insistently men whom we know to be spies); it even allows us to become involved with the spies' projects and see these from their viewpoint . . . The casting of Radford and Wayne could be taken as defusing the urgency of the message, accustomed as we are to smile indulgently at them. Instead it works to wipe the smiles off our faces, to make us look more rigorously at what our acceptance of certain stereotyped images of Britishness may involve us in.

These examples need to be considered in relation to Churchill's known film preferences, of which one will serve as an illustration. When his old friend Alexander Korda announced a film about Nelson and Emma Hamilton, to be made in the United States in 1940, Churchill immediately telegrammed his support for the project. The resulting *Lady Hamilton* (1941), with its rhetorical patriotism and clear pointing of historical parallels between Bonaparte and Hitler, greatly pleased Churchill. According to Korda's biographer, 'he saw the film innumerable times (for the fifth time when he arranged for it to be screened on board the *Prince of Wales* as it took him to the Atlantic Conference in August 1941) and was, by all reports, emotionally moved at every screening.'[9]

That Churchill should prefer the straightforward romantic patriotism of a *Lady Hamilton* to the cautionary ambivalence of *Next of Kin* or *Blimp* is perhaps not surprising. But that he should oppose so tenaciously films which warned against the complacency and inefficiency of the British officer class is surely symptomatic. Churchill's determination to put the war effort above all other considerations is of course well-documented. Lord Ismay, his Chief of Staff from 1940-5, later wrote: 'He was inconsiderate . . .to all of us — but he was far more inconsiderate to himself. The only thing he thought of was the war. Whether anyone was made uncomfortable, or whether he was made extremely uncomfortable, didn't matter a damn.' Such an overriding concern with war priorities might have made him sympathetic to critical propaganda, but it would be a mistake to see Churchill as merely the consumate man of action: he was also possessed by an intense personal — some might say mystical — identification with the war experience, which he communicated in impassioned radio broadcasts. At the height of the bombing of western and south-western ports in May 1941, he felt 'encompassed by an exaltation of spirit in the people which seemed to lift mankind . . . into the joyous serenity we think belongs to a better world than this.'[10] Churchill apparently believed that the role of the media, like his own, was to exhort and inspire, not to criticise or point out shortcomings in the war effort. And as Tom Harrisson noted, 'by appointing his friend Brendan Bracken as fourth and last Minister of Information, after the Blitz, he belatedly imposed his own concept of resolution upon government.[11]

The basis of Churchill's propaganda thrust was an idealised concept of 'the people' welded into 'one nation'; united in suffering and defiance; with class divisions, historical allegiances, even regional distinctions, all dissolved in their stand against the 'common enemy'. To the extent that *Blimp* singled out a military caste, with its dangerously antiquated traditions and values, still in control, it was bound to provoke his antagonism. He may even have seen in the schematic portrait of Clive Candy some resemblance to his own character and career. The American General Lee was not the only wartime observer to detect something Blimpish about Churchill.

4. *Propaganda for Whom?*

In his useful article on 'Propaganda',[12] Steve Neale characterises the 'liberal position' on propaganda, which is indeed the position that has largely constituted our concept, in the following terms: propaganda is a 'vehicle for ideas', which are launched in a calculated assault on the audience with the intention of forcing it to accept a particular ideology. The terms predicated by this model are all more or less 'fixed' in relation to one another: the *intention* and *effect* of propaganda are assumed to account for its operation, with ideology understood vaguely as a 'ghost in the machine'. Thus propaganda becomes an inherently pejorative concept: since it seeks to 'impose' an 'ideology', it is clearly incompatible with liberal humanism, which professes no ideological investment. Faced with the intractability of this position and its confused assumptions, Neale proceeds to re-cast the problematic of propaganda, making use of recent theoretical work on the production of subjectivity and 'subject position', and on ideology. He demonstrates that a proper understanding of the effectivity of propaganda must take account of both the modes of address of the text, and the institutions and apparatuses which at the same time determine textual production and the subject of address. His conclusion is that 'propaganda cannot simply be identified with one particular mode of its problematic of address — dogmatism — and thus dismissed as such, and . . . that the identification of any one text as propaganda can never simply be a matter of the reading off of a set of textual characteristics.' Drawing on Neale's analysis, it is possible to see how *Blimp* could be situated in relation to the contemporary machinery of propaganda, and also why it provoked such controversy.

Although it appeared as an 'entertainment film', two features of the film's textual system are identifiably 'propagandist'. First, the narrative strategy of the framing sequences, which bring the young Army officer into direct conflict with General Candy before moving into the explanatory flashback thus motivated, is contructed so as to place the spectator in a position of dissonance, or conflict — and as Neale observes, 'propaganda as a form of textual address produces a position of social struggle' (p.32). Second, in the opening Turkish Bath exchange and at other points throughout the film, the *mis en scene* produces moments of 'direct address' (through sustained close-up and devices of symmetry) which, by their similarity to other contemporary texts (official exhortations, testimonies by refugees, journalism, etc) would immediately connect with notions of propaganda. However, the crucial point is that neither of these 'propagandist' textual strategies works to align the spectator unambiguously with one or other 'side' of the opposition; the 'subject positions'[13] produced by the text in this particular conjuncture remain sites of contradiction, or at least dissonance. (Thus the young officer is 'right' to denounce Candy's genteel sportsmanship in the context of total war, *but* his 'invasion' and armed threat have overtones of fascist aggression; again, Theo is 'right' to mock Candy's friends as he tells his fellow prisoners-of-war returning to Germany in 1918 that the British naively intend to 'have Germany on its feet again', *but* he is speaking of the post-war situation out of which Hitler and the Nazi party arose, etc).

An assessment of the conjuncture within which *Blimp* was produced and distributed would reveal other contradictions and inscriptions of ideology within the text. For instance, the complexity of Anglo-American-Soviet relations by 1942 had radically transformed the relatively simple propaganda aims of the early war years (see Appendix). The need to develop an 'allied' ideology, and to counteract the cynicism which greeted crude 'hortatory' propaganda, were already producing a more sophisticated approach which was inevitably critical of earlier stereotypes. Again, it is important to realise that there was serious concern at this time in government circles about the relatively low prestige of the Army, as compared with the other services. Churchill's references to 'morale' and 'discipline' in his correspondence with Bracken can almost certainly be related to this concern and the efforts being made to generate propaganda on behalf of the Army.

Other elements of the conjuncture have an even more direct relevance to *Blimp*, for 'Colonel Blimp', as the protagonist of David Low's cartoons in the London *Evening Standard*, was an important focus of dissent from the

Churchillian ideology of 'one nation'. A 1941 cartoon, titled 'Blimp's War for Democracy', shows the Colonel in full armour, flanked by other Blimps in the uniforms of different periods, addressing a civil servant from the Ministry of War:[14]

> Gad, Margesson, we must uphold the leadership of the wealthy classes. After all, we can't waste these uniforms which went with the baronial halls these gentlemen's fathers bought with their profits out of the last war. Tradition, old country families — what? Gad, breeding will tell.

In the following year, Robert Graves published a humorous essay, 'Colonel Blimp's Ancestors', which was suggested 'by the uncomfortable feeling that the British Army still contained far too many pig-headed officers, left overs from the First World War. The essay is a fantasy obituary of the current Colonel, tracing the family from Saxon times, and it ends: 'but this son is still alive and, I regret to say, still on the active list.'[15]

Reading *Blimp* in terms of its specific textual address and within the conjuncture, it becomes clear that it ran a considerable risk of being interpreted as 'negative propaganda' — indeed this was evidently how Churchill, Bracken and other politicians did see it. David Low remarked in an interview at the time of its release: 'Blimp is a symbol of stupidity and stupid people are not necessarily hateful. In fact, some stupid people are quite nice.'[16] By means of a careful deployment of the two terms of identification, Candy and Kretschmar-Schuldorff, the spectator is drawn into a structure of pathos, which implies neither a simple, single 'truth', nor a homogeneous response. In a sense, the space opened up by *Blimp* allows much of what was repressed by 'official' propaganda to emerge and achieve symbolisation: the continuing power of the military-aristocratic class; the political ignorance and prejudice of that class, their philistinism; the heirarchical structure of British society, with its blind deference to age and privilege; the lack of preparation for the war and continuing failure to understand what was at stake. At the same time, the film conspicuously infringes certain codes of propaganda: as the Secretary of State for War points out in his first report, 'the thug element in the make up of the German soldier is ignored'; and the forbidden figure of the 'good German' is introduced, not merely as a 'grateful refugee', but as a critic of British amateurishness and insularity.

Implicitly, *Blimp* also mobilises criticism of the platitudes and misconceptions of official propaganda. While incorporating distinct propaganda moments within its textual scheme, it sets these in play against the relative autonomy of the 'entertainment film'. In view of its openness and heterogeneity, it is hardly surprising that not only officials, but journalists, found it highly perplexing.[17]

116

5. Fantasy and History

> History is the subject of a structure whose site is not homogeneous, empty time, but time filled by the presence of the now.
>
> Walter Benjamin (Spring 1940)[18]

Contemporary British reviewers of *Blimp* were either uncertain of its *meaning* (Lejune: 'what is it *really* about?'), or uncertain that it *had* a meaning (*Tribune:* 'no-one decided *exactly* what they wanted to say with it'). Few shared Brendan Bracken's certainty that it was an 'evident fantasy'; instead they puzzled over its intentions and effects, according to the classic propaganda model discussed above, which is also the classic model of the realist literary text. But the modernist theory of the literary text denies that it is the vehicle of its author's intentions: rather, it is 'a multi-dimensional space in which a variety of writings, none of them original, blend and clash' (Barthes [19]). If we consider the 'textual space' of *Blimp,* it soon becomes clear that this cannot be regarded as a conventional realist narrative. Not only is it heavily marked by the *fantastic,* but the trajectory and dynamic of the narrative is not that of the protagonist(s), but rather of *history.* Despite its contemporaneity, its indices of 'here and now', the space is actually occupied by a fantasy of history — not an individual fantasy, a subjective history, but a 'collective' fantasy which allows the spectator, like Blimp, to 'plunge' back into the history of the previous half-century, and selectively re-work its themes and material.

The function of fantasy as/in history in this context is to orchestrate the elements at play in what has been termed 'popular memory'[20]; to hold together contradictory representations of the forces which provoked war and the subjective experience of a specific historical moment, the war experience itself. Only by introducing the aesthetic strategies characteristic of the fantastic (e.g. the 'floating' relationship between individual characters and their social ground; the possibility of contravening the unity of time and place in favour of a more mythical treatment of time, allowing for the inscription of timelessness, cyclical recurrence, and so forth) can the realist text engage with the representation of abstract concepts such as culture and history and their internal dynamic on a non-personal and yet culturally specific level. However, the *problem* for the text is how to maintain the binding of the spectator through identification, while introducing the discourses of fantasy. (See John Ellis's discussion of a similar problem in relation to *A Matter of Life and Death*).

Several convergent strategies are adopted in *Blimp* to cope with this problem. There is firstly the massive 'fold' in the narrative, which plunges us back into the past in search of 'clues' to the present, a kind of analytic quest. Then there is the recurrent, a-historical figure of 'the woman', played by the same actress (Deborah Kerr) on the three occasions of her appearance. That this is an allegorical representation of 'Britain' (Britannia?) seems inescapable; and such a reading is supported by the 'heraldic' image of the credit sequence (a tapestry of Blimp) and the insertion of the mythological play *Ulysses*.[21] So, we are offered an *allegorical reading* which has Blimp distracted from service in the Empire (South Africa) by the call to defend Britain's honour in Europe (Edith); honour is satisfied, but not rewarded; further service in the Empire, then WW1, which Blimp views as an essentially chivalric passage of arms; after which he again seeks fulfilment in the Empire (the marriage to Barbara). When the imperial mission is ended by death, Blimp returns home to rest on his laurels, but is roused from his dotage by the need to fight again (Angela, his MTC driver). As governess, nurse, wife (the marriage is covered almost entirely by ellipsis — dates, places and momentos), and servicewoman — the woman constantly 'eludes' Blimp, who becomes a figure of impotence. Thus the allegorical discourse points to a possible psychoanalytic reading, which would begin from the remarkable tableau of virility/impotence enacted in the Turkish Bath sequence, when the armed soldiers threaten the unclothed elderly officers. However, because of the layered texture of the film, other readings are also possible and can be constructed on the trace of motivations, specific clues distributed throughout the film, to read in conunction with, or 'against', the various discourses surrounding the film. For instance, we have already noted how the diegetic world of the film includes the 'real' contemporary folk (anti-)hero, Colonel Blimp, who is 'inscribed' by means of the *title* and the one emblematic moment of Candy's resemblance to Blimp in the bath. Should we not also read the central couple of Candy and Kretschmar-Schuldorff as a mode of inscription of the film's authors, Powell and Pressburger, the refugee intellectual and the conventional Englishman?

If *Blimp* is open to such readings, then its 'meaning' and 'intention' were perhaps inevitably enigmatic to contemporary spectators. As an epic representing a view of British history and culture, the film necessarily relied on an activation of national mythology ('popular memory' reformulated through a specific set of ideologies in play during the war). As the project of the text was to represent this history in terms of its contradictions, this dictated a recourse to aesthetic strategies which exceeded the limits of the classic realist text but, by that same token, the text became open to, and was crossed by, those processes of meaning production characteristic of fantasy as a specific signifying process. So, in effect, Blimp became a layered text, where discourses on history, culture, ideologies, sexuality etc, doubled over issues about 'Britishness' and war; the whole constrained but not contained by the framework of plotted inter-relations between a set of characters. In a sense, one can argue that it is the very success of the film in proposing such a complex treatment of history which was responsible for the incomprehension with which it was received at the time. The 'excess' of the film — the extent to which it overflowed the limits of the classic realist text, introduced discourses usually censored both from propagandist modes of address and from conventional realist fictions — came to constitute an enigma, a source of 'trouble', as well as fascination and pleasure for critics and audiences. Reviewers were understandably disturbed by its (then) remarkable length, and by the 'excess' of Technicolor, which can now be seen as aspects of its 'textual productivity'.

Blimp is an *epic* in several rather different senses of the term: while its scope and dramaturgy recall Brecht's epic theatre, it also functions as a 'national epic', incorporating its authors, its audiences (then and now), their history, their culture. Now, with the relevation of Churchill's attempts to suppress it, the full text of *Blimp* continues its acitivity of production, its play of contradictions: it produces new meanings which, in turn, interact with the meanings of 1943, to continually revise and re-produce our idea of history.

NOTES
1.   Raymond E Lee, *The London Observer: A Wartime Journal 1940-1* (London 1972).
2.   I am indebted to Lawrence Hayward for drawing my attention to these and other documents in the Public Record Office.
3.   According to the National Film Archive, some hundred small-scale cuts, as well as major structural changes, have been restored. At the time of writing, the most complete version of the film is a composite nitrate print of about 158 mins (as compared with the original 163 mins). It is hoped to produce an integral full-length negative in the near future.
4.   Interview with Kevin Gough-Yates, BFI 1971.
5.   PRO File INF 1 1978, on the role of the Ministry of Information in wartime censorship.
6.   In an interview with the author.
7.   Michael Balcon, *Michael Balcon Presents . . . A Lifetime of Films* (London 1969), pp 132-6.
8.   Charles Barr, *Ealing Studios* (London 1977), p 28.
9.   Karol Kulik, *Alexander Korda: The Man Who Could Work Miracles* (London 1975), p 249.
10.   Tom Harrisson, *Living Through the Blitz* (London 1976), p 211.
11.   *op cit*, p 282-3.
12.   *Screen*, vol 18 n 3, Autumn 1977.
13.   See the preceding article by John Ellis for an extensive discussion of this concept.
14.   David Low, *The War Cartoons* (London 1941).
15.   The essay appears in a collection, *Occupation: Writer* (London 1949), from the preface of which the introductory remark is quoted.
16.   Quoted in a review in *Time* 2.4.45, on the occasion of the American release.

17. The *Time* review, and an earlier news item in the same magazine (21.6.43) contrast sharply with British press responses. Whereas *Time* found much to admire in the film — and was amused by the outraged British press ('which led other Britons to wonder if Blimp was dead after all') — British film reviewers were mostly puzzled, irritated or grudgingly impressed by the *spectacle* of *Blimp*. It is interesting to note that another admirer of the film was Jean-Pierre Melville: in the *Midi-Minuit Fantastique* interview of 1968, Tavernier and Prayer inform Powell that Melville considers it one of the greatest films. A comparison between *Blimp* and *Armee des Ombres* might be useful.

18. Walter Benjamin, *Illuminations*. 'Theses on the Philosophy of History' XIV, (London 1970), p 263.

19. Roland Barthes, 'The Death of the Author'. *Image-Music-Text* (New York 1977), p 146.

21. David Low's preface to his early war cartoons, an ironic political essay, ends with a proposal for an allegorical war memorial: 'The war memorial this time should be the Dead Past. The deceased died from natural causes during the last war, but is only just becoming aware of it. One of those florid compositions full of detail, after the Westminster Abbey School, featuring National Sovereignty, a goddess festooned in flags with umbrella up to keep off bombs. On her right, a majestic figure of Industry carrying a toolbag symbolic of Production; on her left, another of Finance bearing a ledger; both with the seats out of their pants. Two cherubs, Boom and Bust, ride a Trade-Cycle in the air above, and in the foreground is the goddess of Plenty, on her arm a cornucopia, from the mouth of which peers a Common Person chewing a Hard-Core-of-Unemployment. A striking monument I think.' (May 1941).

Appendix

Programme for Film Propaganda ¹

1. This memorandum assumes the importance of films as a medium of propaganda. It follows the principles outlined in Lord Macmillan's memorandum to the War Cabinet with such changes as are made necessary by adapting abstract ideas to the concrete, dramatic and popular medium of the films. An appendix sets out the same conclusions in practical form.
2. The Themes of our propaganda (Minister's memorandum 4) are:—
   I.   What Britain is fighting for.
   II. How Britain fights.
   III. The need for sacrifices if the fight is to be won.
3. I. *What Britain is fighting for.* This can be treated in
   (a) Feature films.
   (b) Documentaries.
   (c) Cartoons.
4. (a) The main objects of feature films can be:—
   (i) *British life and character,* showing our independence, toughness of fibre, sympathy with the under-dog, etc. *Goodbye Mr. Chips* is an obvious example of this kind. But British characteristics are perhaps more acceptable (especially in the U.S.A.) when less obviously stressed e.g., in *The Lady Vanishes.* In this category we may also consider films of heroic actions, histories of national heroes (Captain Scott) etc., although these may easily become too obvious.
   (ii) *British ideas and institutions.* Ideals such as freedom, and institutions such as parliamentary government can be made the main subject of a drama or treated historically. It might be possible to do a great film on the history of British Liberty and its repercussions in the world (Holland in the 17th, France in the 18th centuries). The value of our institutions could also be brought home to us by showing what it would be like to have them taken away, e.g., a film about a part of the British Isles (e.g. Isle of Man) that the Germans had cut off, showing the effect of the Gestapo on everyday life, breaking up the family, taking away liberties hitherto unnoticed. The 'knock on the door and tap on the shoulder' motif could come in here as well as the next section.

(iii) *German ideals and institutions in recent history.* This might include an historical film of the growth of PanGerman ideas from Bismark onwards. There should be a number of themes for films in the activities of the Gestapo stressing, as more easily credible, the sinister rather than the sadistic aspect, but the Germans should also be shown as making absurd errors of judgement. There should be room for several refugee films, some of which might end in England for contrast; e.g., heavy step, knock on the door, automatic wave of fear, enter an English policeman.

5. (b) *Documentaries.* This treatment of British life and institutions has been the subject of a number of films in the last few years, and it should not be necessary to add greatly to their number. Moreover the projection abroad of British culture is primarily the work of the British Council who have a considerable grant for films.. The chief use of documentaries in propaganda is noted below II (b).

6. (c) *Animated Cartoons.* These are a very flexible medium of propaganda and have the advantage that ideas can be inserted under cover of absurdity. They can present (as in Mickey Mouse) a system of ethics in which independence and individuality are always successful, bullies are made fools of, the weak can cheek the strong with impunity, etc. With a slight twist they can be made topical without being recognisable as propaganda. There are several artists in England who can do them really well.

7. II. *How Britain fights.* This also can be treated in
   (a) Feature films
   (b) Documentaries
   (c) News Reels

8. (a) *Feature Films* of the present war **are alrea**dy being made by private companies (Note: *The Lion Has Wings* may be reckoned as three documentaries strung together to attain feature length. This is its principal defect). A film on *Contraband*[2] is well under way; another on *Convoys* has been begun, a third on **Minesweepers** is in preparation. In all these the documentary element is made part of a dramatic story. Similar treatment should be given to the Army, the Indian war effort, and to one or more of the Dominions. An important feature film could deal with the good relations of French and English troops in France.

9. (b) *Documentaries* A long series should be undertaken to show this country, France and the neutrals the extent of our war effort. There should be, in the first place, full and carefully worked out films of each of the fighting services; then shorter films of all the immediately subsidiary services, i.e., merchant navy, munitions, shipbuilding, coastal command, fishermen, etc. Most of these subjects are susceptible of detailed treatment from different angles, e.g., one-reel films on the Bren Gun, the training of an anti-aircraft gunner, etc. The change from peace to war time conditions should be shown in a whole series drawn from every department of State, e.g. the Ministry of Transport provides the following subjects:—

   Railways — the change over, night work, troop movements, evacuees, etc.

   Roads — lorries at night, bridges ready to be replaced in case

122

of damage, etc.

Ports — control and diversion (a model of the port control room could be built)

Canals — their gradual return to use.

Other Departments (e.g. Agriculture, Education, Health, Home Security, etc.) will provide subjects in the same ratio so that ultimately there should be a complete survey of the Government's war effort.

10. (e) *News Reels.* The selection and proper presentation of news reel material is one of the most vital factors in propaganda. At present the five newsreel companies in France have to pool their results and submit to censorship, but no effort is made to direct their initial policy of selection. This system is wasteful for the newsreel companies (they may have three cameramen on the same spot) and results in trouble with the censorship. It is therefore highly desirable that they should be asked to agree to a plan by which the selection and arrangement of all newsreel material was in the hands of a single office controlled by the Film Division. In this way it would be possible to treat the news in a manner both more coherent and more in keeping with our common aims. The news reel material so produced would then be handed to the five companies to comment on and distribute. Failing this is it absolutely necessary to persuade the five companies to create a single, fortnightly cine-magazine of selected British news for distribution to France and neutrals.

11. *The need for sacrifice if the fight is to be won.* This cannot be made the subject of separate treatment but must be emphasised in certain of the foregoing: e.g. in I (a) (i) British character must be shown as capable of great sacrifices; in I (a) (ii) British insitutions must be shown as having been won and retained by sacrifices; in I (a) (iii) the refugee films should show our sacrifices as trifling compared to the hardships suffered by a defeated people. The sections II (a) and (b), *How Britain fights,* must stress the sacrifices made by merchantmen, fishermen (as minesweepers) and, in documentaries, by railwaymen and all classes of workers. These sacrifices can be shown not as something which the Government is afraid to ask, and the public expected to resent, but as something to be accepted with courage and pride.

12. Apart from this general scheme of film propaganda, the Government will often wish to use the film as an immediate means of communication with the people, e.g., to prevent gossip, to induce greater caution in pedestrians, to explain the shortage of food, etc. These urgent needs are best served by short dramatic films on the model of the American *Crime Does Not Pay* series. They can be quickly made and have a wide appeal. Cartoon films, which are a useful medium of communication, cannot generally be used for this purpose as they take too long to make.

13. Before passing to the practical examination of this programme in the appendix, certain general principles of film propaganda remain to be stated.

14. The same treatment is not equally valid at home, on the Continent, in the U.S.A. and in the Dominions. For example, pictures of English liberty and honour welcomed at home are interpreted on the Continent as evidence of slackness and stupidity. Shots of our soldiers laughing or

playing football must be cut out of all newsreels and documentaries sent to France. So sharp is the division that it will be necessary to make documentary films specially for France and neutral countries. For many neutrals specially prepared cine-magazines will be necessary. Feature films will often have to be cut, or given alternative endings to bring them into consonance with local feelings.

15. The film being a popular medium must be good entertainment if it is to be good propaganda. A film which induces boredom antagonises the audience to the cause which it advocates. For this reason, an amusing American film with a few hits at the Nazi regime is probably better propaganda than any number of documentaries showing the making of bullets, etc.

16. This leads to the further consideration that film propaganda will be most effective when it is least recognisable as such. Only in a few rare prestige films, reassurance films and documentaries should the Government's participation be announced. The influence brought to bear by the Ministry on the producers of feature films, and encouragement given to foreign distributors must be kept secret. This is particularly true of any films which it is hoped to distribute in America and other neutral countries, which should in some instances actually be made in America and distributed as American films.

17. This programme deals only with production. It will be remembered, however, that an almost equally important part of the Film Division's duty is the effective distribution throughout the world of all films showing British life and the war effort. The problems of distribution differ in each country and it is only possible to state one general principle: that theatrical distribution through ordinary commercial channels is incomparably more effective, although more difficult to achieve, than distribution through diplomatic or other private agencies.

1. This document is from the Ministry of Information papers held by the Public Record Office (File INF 1/867). Although it is unsigned and undated, the reference to Lord Macmillan and other clues suggest that it dates from early 1940. Macmillan was the first Minister of Information (September 1939-January 1940); followed by Reith; then Duff Cooper from May 1940; and finally, from July 1941 for the rest of the war, Bracken. The Appendix referred to is not available.

2. This is obviously a reference to Powell and Pressburger's *Contraband*, which was trade shown in March 1940.